SPEND ON YOUR FUTURE

Investing and Money Management Made Easy

Tim D. Collins   Jane D. Lehr

Orca
Books
Publishing

Published by:

Orca Books Publishing
2947 76th Avenue S.E., Suite 92D
Mercer Island, WA 98040
(206) 230-9093;
Fax: (206) 236-1209

Copy Editor: Kerry Colburn Tessaro
Cover Design by: Presentations Northwest, Seattle, WA

Cataloging in Publication Data

Collins, Tim D.
   Spend On Your Future: Investing and Money
Management Made Easy / Tim D. Collins and Jane D. Lehr.
        p. cm.
   Includes Glossary
   1. Investments. 2. Personal Finance. I. Title.
   332.678

ISBN 0-9639889-3-X

"This is the best primer book I have ever read. I consider myself a fairly sophisticated investor and I learned from it." — James Healy, Healy Associates

"I never have been able to finish an investing book until I read *Spend On Your Future*. Its step-by-step approach is easy to understand and read." — Chris Parker, Teacher

"After reading *Spend On Your Future*, I spent $300 on *my* future. I know it's not much, but it's a start." — Eric Blohm, Sales Representative

"As a husband who wants to provide for my family, it's necessary to know how to get a head start in spending for our future. This book has opened my eyes to the value of investing." — Joe Soucy, Firefighter

"I am a person who was never interested in investing, but this book showed me that investing isn't just for retirement." — Emily Short, Director of Marketing and Public Relations, Rose Villa, Inc.

"I never realized that some investments only require a small amount of money to begin. *Spend On Your Future* gave me the encouragement to begin investing." — Tricia Fejfar, Child Therapist

"I would recommend this book to anyone who wants to put their hard-earned dollar to work for them." — Patrick Hoey, Account Manager

CONTENTS

Foreword:

You already have what it takes to invest successfully. By possessing common sense, you are halfway there. This book will walk you through different investments, along with the concepts, strategies, and reminders you need to know, in a language we all understand. We purposefully kept several topics brief to include only what you *need* to know to get started. We realize that you do not want a Ph.D. in Finance, you just want to learn how to make your money work for you. Other beginning investment books will make you believe that it takes $1,000 or more to begin investing beyond a savings account, but that is not true. This book will change the way you think about investing.

We dedicate this book to everyone who has ever struggled to get through an investing and money management book, to those who have slept through numerous financial planning seminars, to those who think their dreams are out of reach, and to those who love to spend money. Say good-bye to investing jargon of the past, and say hello to investing, "spending style."

INTRODUCTION

Somewhere along the way, the high volume traders and big dollar account managers forgot how to explain **investing** basics to beginning and amateur investors. Many experts have written books, given seminars, and developed what they claim to be "easy to follow" investment plans, which in reality few individuals can follow. By using words such as "forced savings" and "mandatory retirement planning," investing brings on a negative mindset and becomes something you have to do. This book will dispel those beliefs and fundamentally change the way you look at investing. Investing is not forced savings, rather, it is spending on your future. After all, everyone is better at spending than saving.

Too often, beginning investors are too intimidated to walk into a brokerage firm, and with good reason. If you don't know the basics of investing, there is a good chance you will lose more than you gain. However, the gains to be had are well worth your interest and attention. Investing is not just for gray-haired men in dark suits and white shirts. Investing is for everyone. Do not be trapped by low interest-bearing accounts when there are many alternatives. From mutual funds, to stocks and bonds, to real estate, this book will introduce you to a host of investment alternatives, many of which require little money to get started.

People who are skilled in investing may not be skilled at explaining the concepts of investing in a language we all understand. Caught up in the investing world and surrounded by people who speak their language, they expect everyone to understand their jargon. For example: "The bear battles the bull and indicators are mixed." "Stocks receive strong support from the recent bond rally spurred by Federal Reserve cuts." "Durable good equities continue to rally upon strong consumer spending levels."

Believe it or not, an experienced investor could make sense of those statements; however, for the rest of us it leaves an impression that investing is only for sophisticated professionals. That is why many people cry "help" when it comes to the mysterious world of investing. But wait a minute. Investing isn't mysterious, and do not let anyone tell you it is. Investing is for anyone who ever made a dollar or stuck a penny in the piggy bank. Once you have learned the basics, investing is as easy as spending money.

This book will dispel the belief that investing is stressful, complicated, migraine-producing, divorce-causing, confusing and worst of all, something you have to do. You will be shown why investing doesn't have to be just another to-do item on the list that is forever stuck on everyone's refrigerator: #9 — take yard waste to city dump, and #10 — invest for the golden years.

Start Spending Now

Whether you have $10, $50, $500, or more, start spending now. Once you start to invest, your money will work for you. Investing works on the **power of compounding**. This means that the earlier you start to invest, the more time your money will have to build upon itself. Think of your money as a snowball. At first it is small, but as you roll it, it becomes larger. The larger it gets, the faster it grows in size. This analogy will apply to your money as well. Take a look at the example below. Even though Susie contributed $55,000 ($100,000 minus $45,000) less than Sam, by starting early she ended up with over $700,000 more.

Both Individuals Are 40 Years From Retirement Both Earn a 10% Return Compounded Annually		At The End Of 40 Years
"Spend Now Susie"	Spends $3,000 a year for the first 15 years and does not contribute thereafter ($45,000).	$1,136,000
"Spend Later Sam"	Waits 15 years before spending, and then contributes $4,000 a year for the last 25 years($100,000).	$432,700
	Difference	$703,300

A benchmark rule to determine how long it will take to double your money is the **"Rule of 72."** The Rule of 72 is a compounding rule that calculates the number of years to double an investment as 72 divided by the interest rate (72 ÷ interest rate = # of years to double an investment). For example, at a 10% interest rate, it would take 7.2 years to double your investment. The following table demonstrates the difference between a 3% and 10% return for a $2,000 per year investment compounded annually. Over 30 years this can really make a difference.

Interest Rate	5 Years	10 Years	15 Years	20 Years	30 Years
3%	$10,937	$23,616	$38,314	$55,353	$98,005
5%	$11,604	$26,414	$45,315	$69,439	$139,522
8%	$12,672	$31,291	$58,649	$98,846	$244,692
10%	$13,431	$35,062	$69,899	$126,005	$361,887

You are probably familiar with investments such as savings accounts and certificates of deposit. Although these make up an important part of your personal finances, some of this money can be allocated to higher yielding investments. In the following chapters you will learn about basic money management skills and many other different types of investments such as mutual funds, stocks, bonds, Treasury securities, retirement investments, precious metals, life insurance and real estate. We will also provide you with Investing's Top Ten Tips and explain some key investment principles such as diversification, monthly investing, matching your objectives, management, risk versus reward, planning, and spending. If these principles seem dry, boring or overly complex, think again, because they will be explained in a lighthearted manner that everyone can understand.

CHAPTER 1

INVESTING'S TOP TEN TIPS

Before beginning with Investing's Top Ten Tips, we want to define the word "tip." Generally, the word "tip" is associated with riskiness, such as a "hot stock tip." Our Top Ten Tips are actually investing concepts and reminders.

We are not going to claim throughout this book that we have made millions overnight in our investments, because we haven't. However, by understanding Investing's Top Ten Tips, we have done well with the investments we have chosen and have built up a comfortable sum of money. Now do not misunderstand. We have also chosen investments that have lost money, but fortunately you can learn from our mistakes. Our first mistake was listening to people who say, "Investing is so simple. Sell

short on Teledax; it never fails." Unfortunately, investments can lose money; do not let anyone tell you
otherwise. However, if you understand the basics of investing, your risk of excessive losses diminishes. If at
any time you forget the definition of a term or run into a
stumbling block, we have included an extensive glossary at the end of this book. It includes all bold face
words found in the text. Let's begin with Investing's
Top Ten Tips:

1) RISK VS. REWARD. The higher the expected
return on any investment, the greater the **risk** an investor
faces. This statement always holds true because the
riskier an investment becomes, the higher the rate of return an institution has to offer in order to lure investors
away from safer places to put their money. For example,
federally insured investments generally offer a lower rate
of return because they are virtually risk-free. If you had
to choose between a federally insured investment offering a 5% rate of return and investing in "Bob's Buffalo
Burger Stand," also offering a 5% expected rate of return, you would always put your money in the insured
investment. In order for you to invest in "Bob's Buffalo
Burger Stand," Bob would have to offer a higher expected
rate of return to compensate for the risk that the public
may not be crazy about buffalo burgers.

Risk is an important part of investing. The investments you choose should match your personal risk profile
and objectives. If you do not consider yourself a big risk
taker (the thought of gambling in Las Vegas puts butter-
flies in your stomach), or if you are looking for a
long-term retirement investment, then you probably
would not invest in Bob's Buffalo Burgers, no matter
what rate of return it offered. You would probably be

better served in a more conservative investment, or at least in having a majority of your savings there. You might be willing to risk 5% of your savings on Bob.

Risk can also be thought of in terms of the following four categories: individual company, industry, domestic economy, and global economy risk. Although you cannot control all types of risk, you must take them into consideration before you decide to invest. These four categories work with each other to form an overall degree of risk. The individual company risk is associated with the financial health of a particular company and its position within the industry. Since companies typically operate within an industry, you also need to be aware of industry risk. A company could be financially strong, but operate in an industry facing upcoming adverse conditions. In this case, the industry might not be attractive to you as an investor. Industry risks are also affected by factors in the domestic economy. Domestic economy risk is associated with the day to day operations of the United States economy. Interest rates, inflation rates, and other factors affect each industry differently. For example, in times of high inflation, the real estate industry often prospers.

Companies work within an industry and domestic economy, but they may also need to compete globally. Therefore, it is important to take notice of world events. Some of these events may have an affect upon your investment. For example, trade agreements between the United States and other countries could allow expansion into new territories or allow additional competition from foreign companies.

2) DIVERSIFICATION. Do not put all of your hard earned income into any one investment. **Diversifi-**

cation is the name of the game. Diversification works to reduce the level of risk in your portfolio. A diversified **portfolio** (investor lingo for your collection of investments) should perform well despite what the economic climate offers. We will talk in more detail on this subject, but it is easy to understand. An investor needs to hedge his or her investment portfolio against volatility in any one industry or investment. Huh? How about "don't put all your eggs in one basket." Do not build your portfolio with all high-tech stocks or all **municipal bonds**.

3) MINIMUM INVESTMENT. A large inheritance is not necessary to begin investing. Although some investments require a minimum investment of anywhere from $1,000 to $10,000 to begin, you can start investing with almost any amount of money. For example, there are many mutual funds (which we will identify in Chapter 4) that require only $25 to $50 to get started. Remember, investing is not only for the rich and famous. It is for anyone who wants to see their hard earned money work for them and not disappear. Chapter 3 offers suggestions on how to decrease your monthly expenditures, and in turn, increase your investing capabilities.

4) MONTHLY SPENDING. Once you make your initial investment, it is important to continue monthly spending on investments. Plan for and spend a specified amount each month. Yes, we said "spend," because we want you to start thinking of investments as purchases. Nobody likes to save money . . . because what's the fun in just saving? In fact, the personal savings rate was 10% in 1975 and 5% in 1990 — a major decline. We belong to a society in which the three favorite words are spend, spend, spend. So go ahead, have fun, buy as many investments as you can afford. Now it might not seem as invigorating as buying a new pair of skis or fancy clothes, and it may not seem as elegant as a night out at your favorite restaurant, but you should feel good about the investments you purchase. The importance of spending each month is demonstrated by the power of compounding which we discussed in the introduction. Over time you will be amazed at how quickly your money grows.

Additionally, by investing the same amount each month, no matter how small, you receive the benefit of a stock market buying strategy called **dollar cost averaging**. When prices are high, your monthly investment buys fewer shares. When share prices are low, your monthly investment buys more shares. In the end, the investor owns the shares at an average price per share between the high and low fluctuations. Over time, as share prices rise, your shares gain in value. This takes the guess work out of the difficult task of timing market fluctuations. Remember, you must invest consistently over long periods of time. Do not invest for two years and quit. Sometimes the market can underperform or overperform. Investing monthly and thinking long-term will reduce the risk of you jumping in and out of the market at the wrong time.

An excellent way to begin investing each month is by direct deposit. You can begin by taking 10% of your paycheck each month and transferring it into an investment account. The benefits of direct depositing are twofold: first, if money is not sitting in your checking account, you can't spend it on something else. Second, this really takes the pain out of writing a check each month. There are banks, brokerage firms, and mutual funds that offer automatic investment plans (direct deposits). You decide how much should be taken out of your regular bank account or paycheck each month and placed in your investment account. For example, you could have a mutual fund investment account and each month a predetermined amount of money will be used to purchase shares in a mutual fund. No worries!

5) EXPERTS. Do not believe everything you hear. There are many experts in the field of financial planning and brokering who have excellent training and experience and can offer good recommendations. However, there are also what we like to term "smooth talkers" of the industry. Because the slick smoothies exist, it is important to know the investing language first; otherwise, you could get talked into an investment that is not right for you. By definition, there is a difference between a **broker** and a **financial planner**, though often the terms are used interchangeably. Both brokers and financial planners can be licensed to buy and sell securities, but financial planners can provide additional investment advice such as retirement planning and goal setting. There are financial planners who charge a fee for the actual planning, but do not purchase the securities. Be sure to ask a broker or financial planner up front about their qualifications and limitations.

One way to protect yourself against unqualified advisors is to research information about the individual's disciplinary record. Investors can call the **National Association of Securities Dealers (N.A.S.D.)** at

1-800-289-9999 to find out whether there have been any disciplinary actions taken against a licensed dealer by state or federal regulators or by groups like N.A.S.D.

6) FORECASTS. No one can accurately predict the future. Financial analysts will gladly give their forecasts for the future because this is their job. There are times these analysts are right, but sometimes they're wrong. Predicting the future of investments is like predicting the weather in the Pacific Northwest. A 20% chance of showers could easily mean a 100% chance of downpours! It also won't take you long to realize that for every analyst that says "up," you can always find one that says "down." If the future could be predicted with certainty, we would all be millionaires. Remember, there is no magic formula for investing. Read this book, follow Investing's Top Ten Tips, and ask for financial planning and brokering advice if you are comfortable with the person giving it. Continue your own research and you will come up with your own successful formula for investing.

7) REFERENCES. Get intimate with the investor's references. It may strike some people as odd that we list investor reading references in the first chapter, but investing references need to be listed up front, to give them the recognition they deserve. Spending time with the references mentioned below is an essential and beneficial part of investing.

There are a number of good magazines that cover current investing topics and general business news, such as *Business Week*, *Forbes*, *Fortune*, *Kiplinger's*, *Money*, *Newsweek*, and *Time*. A majority of these magazines also publish a specific mutual fund issue, where they rank different funds. It is in your best interest to sneak off into a corner once or twice a month and update yourself on what is happening in the business world. What are the analysts, fund managers and economists preaching this month? Which are the booming industries and which industries are contracting? What are the hot topics and how will they affect your investment? This does not mean choking down every sentence of every article, but it does pay to do some heavy browsing.

Additional reference publications that will help you analyze investment choices include *The Wall Street Journal*, *Moody's Investors Service*, *Value Line Investment Survey*, *Morningstar Mutual Funds*, *Standard &Poor's*, *Barron's Finance and Investment Handbook,* and *Robert Morris & Associates Annual Statement Studies.* Of course, this is not an all inclusive list. This may sound like a lot of dry reading, but the following chapters, will provide easy ways to quickly evaluate investments using these publications. We will also take you through a financial analysis of a hypothetical company. All of these references, plus more, can be purchased or are available for free browsing at your local library.

Also at the library are two excellent investor references: the computerized Compact Disclosure (CD) system and the InfoTrac system. The Compact Disclosure system contains annual report data on over 12,000 public U.S. companies. Typing in a company name will instantly bring up financial statements, stock and dividend information, the names of senior company executives, the individuals or investment groups that own a majority of the stock, and various pieces of other financial information.

The InfoTrac system contains newspaper and magazine articles. It provides information on numerous companies and executives. Both systems are available at many local libraries and bring a wealth of company information to your fingertips. Do not worry if you feel uneasy using a computer; the programs are easy to learn and there are always helpful librarians that will provide assistance. We will discuss throughout this book why these tidbits of information are so valuable!

8) THINK. Before handing over any money, you should always — and we repeat always — research and give each investment thorough personal thought. After all, you are now spending on your future. Think about each company's products and/or services. . . are they good? Would you buy them? Which industries are involved in a particular fund? Are they growing or contracting? These are examples of questions that may lead you to an investment. These questions, along with the references we have cited above, can help distinguish a profitable investment from a loser. *Do not let anyone talk you into an investment without first seeing financial information on paper.*

9) TAXES. When investing, it is important not to forget about Uncle Sam and the Internal Revenue Service. Any investment you choose will have tax implications. Investments can be tax-free or tax-advantaged in the form of deferments, deductions or credits. For example, municipal bonds are fully exempt from federal income tax and in many cases exempt from state and local taxes. In Chapter 8, we will discuss tax advantaged investments and show you how much of a difference taxes make to your total return on investment.

10) YOU CAN DO IT! Last, but most important, remember that you can do it. Incorporate the concepts and reminders provided in Investing's Top Ten Tips into your investing objectives. Devote time to your investment decisions and think of investing as a lifelong opportunity. We know it is not as exciting as buying a new red convertible, but it can be fun and it doesn't have to be stressful. Use your best judgment on what makes sense to you. Peter Lynch, author of *Beating The Street* and *One Up On Wall Street*, states ". . . an amateur who devotes a small amount of study to companies in an industry he or she knows something about can out-perform 95% of the paid experts who manage the mutual funds — plus have fun doing it." YOU CAN DO IT!

<u>Recap of Investing's Top Ten Tips</u>

1. The higher the expected rate of return, the greater the risk.
2. Diversify your investments.
3. You can begin investing with little money.
4. Plan for and spend a specified amount each month on investments.
5. Know the basics of investing *before* talking to a financial planner or stockbroker.
6. No one can accurately predict the future.
7. Get intimate with investor's references.
8. Always research an investment before opening your wallet.
9. Don't forget the tax implications on different investments.
10. YOU CAN DO IT!

CHAPTER 2

DEFINING GOALS / DREAMS

You should be wary of anyone offering pre-packaged investment advice, because good investing is not a generic item that can be given to a group of people. An investing portfolio should be tailored to an individual to meet his or her needs, goals, and dreams. This chapter should encourage you to design your portfolio to match your specific objectives. It is likely that your portfolio will include a balance of investments from conservative, to moderately risky, to a small percentage in higher risk investments.

Investors with many years of earning potential are

usually encouraged to invest a majority of their portfolio for long-term growth. This can be found in several different investments such as real estate, or mutual funds and stocks which pay little or no **dividends** (payments). These investments are structured for future growth because they reinvest the dividends back into the company. Investors who are closer to retirement are usually encouraged to invest a majority of their portfolio in investments that supplement their income. This could be accomplished through many investment vehicles such as bonds which pay interest, or mutual funds and stocks that pay high dividends. The following chapter will provide you with some examples of goals and dreams to help you develop your own.

Before diving into the first mutual fund or stock tip you learned about from your best friend's mother's second cousin, spend some quality time planning. Think of it as preparation for a vacation. Pretend the infamous "two weeks" (that is never enough) is approaching and time must be spent in planning whether you will be putting your toes in the sand or shredding moguls on the ski hill. Investing requires the same type of planning. We know what you're saying: "I just want to invest, be a high roller, make $10 million overnight and sail away on a 60-foot sailboat down to the Caribbean." Our response to you is to turn off your television and stop listening to individuals who preach instant success and overnight financial independence. Start now, utilize the power of compounding and determine — on your own or after discussion with those closest to you — what you want your investments to accomplish.

You have access to investments that can make money and work for you. We know everyone works hard for their money, so why would you let your money sit watching T.V. all day while you work your fingers to the bone? Make your investments work twenty-four hours a day. Go ahead, be a slave driver, but first decide what your investments should do. Sorry, they don't do windows, but they can, for instance, provide a secure retirement.

Goals

Retirement may seem a long way off to you now, but it is your most important investment today. Take the pain out of investing for retirement and start small, but start today. As discussed earlier, the power of compounding will make it easier for you to attain your retirement goals. Chapter 8 will discuss the different investments you can choose for your retirement. Even though your friends and family love you very much, they might think it an imposition for you to move in for your retirement years because you have squandered your life savings. If you are relying on social security to guide you down "Easy Street" through retirement, think again. There is a good chance you will not see every dollar that you have contributed. In less than 20 years from now, depending on their salaries, retiring individuals can expect to receive approximately 60% to 80% of what they put in. The social security percentage is only going to go lower; if you haven't already started planning for the golden years, there is no time like the present. This is not meant to imply that retirement begins at age 65. With prudent investing, depending upon your personal goals, it may begin earlier. After all, who wants to spend their whole life working?

In addition to a retirement investment, you will need to keep a portion of your portfolio in liquid investments, regardless of your age. A liquid investment, contrary to popular belief, is not an investment in orange juice commodities. When an investment is **liquid**, it means that it can quickly be converted into cash within a short period of time with little or no penalty or cost. A savings account is an example of a liquid investment. You can withdraw cash at any time of the day without incurring a penalty. It is necessary to have liquid investments for life's little emergencies. It is a standard recommendation to keep between 5% - 15% of your total investments in cash or highly liquid investments.

Don't forget the loved ones surrounding you. If you have any children, and would someday like to get them out of the house and into college (mostly out of the house), you will need to have the funds available for them when that time arrives. Over the past 15 years, college costs have risen an average of 8.4% annually. In terms of your wallet, that means costs will double every eight years. One wise man told us that the cost of college is nothing compared to the cost of a wedding. Needless to say, he has five daughters, but these types of future costs need to be planned for today. If your children will need a sizable sum of money in the future, do not procrastinate until it is too late. Once your child is born, an additional standard deduction can be taken on your tax return. Why not take the tax you would have paid on the standard deduction amount and invest in your child's future?

Dreams

Once your goals have been determined, the next step is to write down your dreams. How about that vacation to Europe next summer, or that new set of golf clubs you've been eyeing for the past six months? Maybe you've always wanted to own a summer cottage on the beach, a condo in Vail or a penthouse in New York City.

Goals	**Dreams**
Retirement	Golf Clubs
Emergency Fund	Vacation
Child's College	Beach House

Regardless of which investments are included in your portfolio, be sure that the investments you have chosen meet your objectives in terms of risk, convenience, liquidity, and diversification. Wow, that's a mouthful and a lot to think about before choosing an investment, but by the end of this book all those terms will seem commonplace and will help you in investing for your dreams and goals.

MONTHLY INVESTING

Any book about investing would be incomplete without a discussion of how to determine the amount to invest each month. You must take a realistic look at what you can afford. Don't worry, you will not have to starve yourself, your dog, or your children; you only have to plan. This means directly depositing money from your checking account to your investment account each month. We know how easily that extra money gets spent. Start small. For example plan to invest 10% of each paycheck, and in months when you have the opportunity, try to increase it to 20% or 30%. Remember, investing is for security, special opportunities, and a better way of life.

Separate your goals and dreams from Chapter 2 into

INVESTMENT CONTRIBUTION PLAN

	Monthly Contribution	Annual Contribution	1993	Year End Goals 1994	1995
Short-Term					
Car Downpayment	$100	$1,200	$1,200	$2,400	$3,600
Stereo	42	500	500	-----	-----
Vacation	125	1,500	1,500	-----	-----
Clothes	50	600	600	-----	-----
Furniture / Housewares	42	500	500	-----	-----
Total	$358	$4,300	$4,300	$2,400	$3,600
Long-Term					
House Downpayment	$250	$3,000	$3,000	$6,000	$9,000
College	25	300	300	600	900
Retirement	167	2,000	2,000	4,000	6,000
Vacation Property	42	500	500	1,000	1,500
Total	$483	$5,800	$5,800	$11,600	$17,400

short-term and long-term. Starting with your goals, determine the amount you can afford to spend each month. You are doing great if you can afford to spend on each of your goals. During months when you have extra income to spend, you can put it towards your dreams. As long as you have started to spend on your goals early, there is no need to contribute more to goals during months of high disposable income. Spend it on your dreams. The work sheet is an example of how you might separate your short-term and long-term goals and dreams. Your total monthly contribution can be spent on any number of different investments. Whether or not the amounts in the example are realistic for you is not important. What is important is to have a plan. You will be surprised how quickly your monthly contributions will add up.

Easy Ways to Increase Monthly Income Without Robbing a Bank

Once you have decided your investment goals and determined the amount you can invest/spend each month, you are well on your way. No matter what your initial monthly investment amount is, there are ways to increase it regardless of your current income level or salary. Here are a few suggestions of ways to reduce your monthly expenditures, and in turn increase the amount of your investments.

1) CHECKING ACCOUNTS & CREDIT CARD FEES. Switch from fee checking accounts and credit cards to no-fee services. Banks and credit card services are in such competition that you can avoid paying monthly (or per check) fees on a simple checking account or credit card by shopping around. There are many credit cards currently being offered with low interest rates and no annual fee. This may not seem like a lot of money, but it can save you up to $100 per year, which, if invested at 8% compounded monthly for twenty years, equals approximately $5,000.

2) CREDIT CARD RATES & TERMS. Choose credit cards with low interest rates and grace periods (time between last purchase and payment date) of 25 days or longer. Believe it or not, there are credit cards that force you to pay 10 days after your last purchase of the month. It is to your advantage to have more days to pay. This allows your money to earn interest for you and not for the credit card. Listed below are four different credit cards with low rates, no annual fees, and grace periods of 25 days. This list can be found each month in *Money* magazine. The chart below is a recent example.

	Example Rates	Telephone #
Oak Brook Bank (Ill)	11.90	800-666-1011
Amalgamated Bank (Ill)	12.00	800-723-0303
AFBA Industrial Bank (Col)	12.50	800-776-2265
Transflorida Bank	12.90	305-434-5111

3) CREDIT CARD FINANCE CHARGES. Pay off your credit card balances. Live within your means. When buying personal goods, spend an amount that you can realistically pay for within one month. You should pay off the total balance due each month and avoid all finance charges. If our advice is coming too late and you already have an excessively large credit card balance, there is another option. If you own your home, you can take out a home equity loan to pay off credit card balances and personal debt. Typically, home equity loan rates are lower than credit card finance rates. Therefore, it is to your advantage to use this option. Another saving feature of a home equity loan (up to $100,000) is that the interest you pay may be deducted on your tax return, so in essence you could save twice. Who can beat that?

4) MONTHLY EXPENSES. Prepare a monthly record of expenses with categories entitled "non-frivolous" and "frivolous." On the next page is a sample work sheet to keep track of weekly expenses. This does not mean that you have to eat oatmeal every morning for breakfast because it only costs pennies a bowl; however, everyone has a few extra frivolous items on which they can cut down. It is easy to spot these items when they are on paper. You do not have to record expenses every month. Do it once or twice to find out where your money goes.

Examples of non-frivolous consumer goods are necessary clothes and drug store items such as prescriptions, toothpaste, etc. Examples of frivolous consumer goods are new clothes for a night on the town or a new bike because you did not like the color of your old one. Be sure to include such expenses as home and car insurance

Week	Housing	Food	Car	Utilities	Consumer Goods	All Other	Subtotal	Consumer Goods	Eating Out	Entertain-ment	All Other	Subtotal	TOTAL
					NON-FRIVOLOUS (I Need)					FRIVOLOUS (I Want)			
1	$180	$85	$85	$25	$35	$10	$420	$55	$40	$25	$10	$130	$550
2	180	75	85	25	40	25	$430	75	25	30	15	$145	$575
3	180	90	85	25	45	5	$430	65	15	55	25	$160	$590
4	180	95	85	25	15	15	$415	45	65	35	20	$165	$580
+	90	35	43	13	10	10	$201	20	10	10	10	$50	$251
May Total	$810	$380	$383	$113	$145	$65	$1,896	$260	$155	$155	$80	$650	$2,546
1	$180	$90	$85	$20	$45	$15	$435	$90	$45	$15	$20	$170	$605
2	180	70	85	20	30	20	$405	75	30	40	20	$165	$570

in your weekly amounts. In the end, you have to decide if an item is frivolous or non-frivolous.

5) MONTHLY PAYCHECK. Lastly, if you always receive a tax refund, you can increase the amount of each paycheck by adjusting your withholding. By law, you are entitled to break even with the I.R.S., not supply the government with extra interest that you should be receiving instead. Increasing the allowances you take on your W-4 form will have the effect of reducing the amount that the government withholds from each paycheck. This in turn increases each paycheck you take home, which means more money available each month to invest. Just ask your employer for a new W-4 and use their work sheet to figure your allowances so that you break even. Be sure to include all of last year's deductions, adjustments to income, deductible IRA, etc. A simple formula to use is to add one allowance for every $600 in refunds received. A note of caution: withhold too little money and you will incur a penalty.

Managing your money is without a doubt the hardest part of investing. Don't get frustrated if at first it appears you are *mangling* your money instead of managing it. It will become easier with experience. For additional help in managing your money look into *The Tightwad Gazette* (Villard Books), by Amy Dacyczyn and *1001 Ways to Cut Your Expenses* (Dell Publishing), by Jonathan D. Pond.

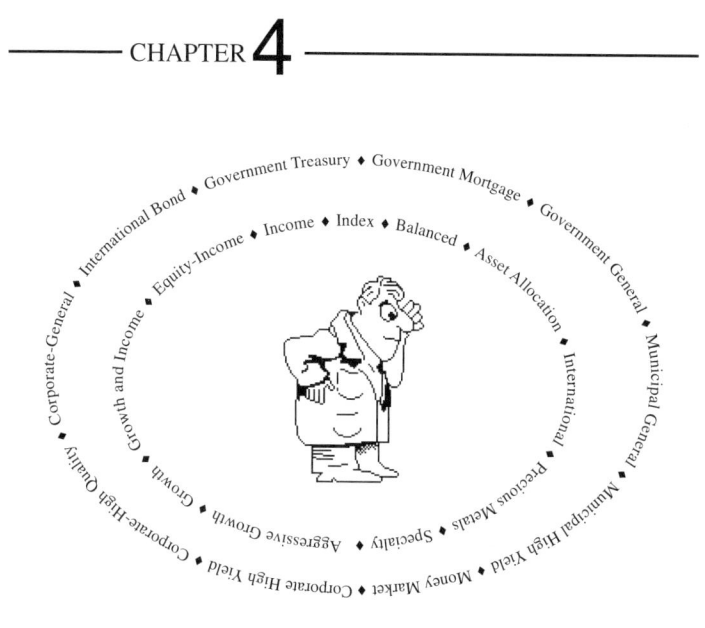

CHAPTER 4

MUTUAL FUNDS

For investors who have a large amount or only a small amount of money to start, mutual funds are a great investment. They can provide you with a level of diversification you might not otherwise attain. However, it should be noted that mutual funds, as with other investments, have varying degrees of risk from conservative to risky. **Mutual funds** pool investors' deposits to buy stocks, bonds, and various other investments.

Recent years have brought a record level of deposits to mutual funds. Investors pour $1 billion dollars into mutual funds each day. The statistics go on and on and the choices of mutual funds are endless. If we stacked each mutual fund on top of each other, the pile would reach from here to the moon. (OK, we made up that statistic.) However, there are well over 2,500 mutual funds available, classified into different investment objective categories. We have listed 21 such categories at the end of this chapter. There is a mutual fund that matches your investment strategy, but how are you supposed to choose? You can either throw darts at the Mutual Fund section in *The Wall Street Journal* or learn the basics of mutual funds. We suggest the latter option.

Choosing a Mutual Fund

Think of a mutual fund as a pizza with tomato sauce. You, the investor, can choose toppings you desire. This means that mutual funds can be customized to fit your investing goals and level of desired risk. Maybe you like all pepperoni or a combination of pepperoni and mushrooms. Just like your pizza, a mutual fund can be made up of a single security such as stocks or contain a combination of securities such as stocks, bonds, and cash. If you choose pepperoni, you must also decide if you want the spicy Italian pepperoni or a milder version. In other words, the stocks or other securities contained in any one mutual fund have a degree of risk associated with them.

Some mutual funds hold investments that have a high degree of risk and offer potentially higher yields. For example, there are funds that invest mainly in small company stocks or technology funds, which seek out small, emerging growth companies. These funds are classified in the "aggressive growth" category. If you need a more conservative investment, you could invest in a "balanced fund," which includes a combination of stocks and bonds. This can provide for better diversification by spreading risk among two different types of securities.

We have just discussed two types of mutual fund categories. The mutual fund categories (listed at the end of this chapter) will assist you in choosing mutual funds that match your objectives. These category explanations are for you to use as a reference tool. Concentrate primarily on researching mutual funds in the categories that fit your needs.

Mutual Fund Families

Mutual funds not only like to group themselves into categories, but they also love to be with their families. It sounds corny, but you will hear the phrase, "**mutual fund family**." Mutual funds are operated by an investment company. These companies provide investors with different categories of funds varying in levels of risk. These different categories are identified by the investment company's name, such as Fidelity or Janus. This is followed by their individual name, such as Fidelity Magellan Fund or Janus Twenty Fund. As an example, look at the Janus family tree.

Janus Funds

Janus Fund	Janus Growth & Income
Janus Twenty	Janus Balanced
Janus Venture	Janus Flexible Income
Janus Enterprise	Janus Short-Term Bond
Janus Worldwide	Janus Intermediate Government Securities

All of these mutual funds have different investing strategies, but they all belong to the same family.

The Love of Mutual Funds

There are several characteristics of mutual funds that appeal to investors. We talked about the importance of diversification, and with many mutual funds it is present to an extent. An equity mutual fund will contain anywhere from 40 to over 1,000 different stocks. This provides diversification in one type of security, but do not forget about diversifying among other securities, such as bonds. This can be accomplished through other types of mutual funds.

Mutual funds also come equipped with professional portfolio managers. These individuals are in charge of choosing what securities to buy and sell for the fund. Chapter 6, Annual Reports and Prospectuses, stresses the importance of researching top level management and their track records. The same tactic applies to mutual funds. Many mutual funds have similar profiles, but it is the person at the helm who can make the difference. As a coach makes a sports team, a professional money manager makes a mutual fund. Peter Lynch, legendary in the financial world, managed the Fidelity Magellan Fund for 13 years, averaging an annual return of 28%. One can hardly pick up a financial magazine and not see his name mentioned. You can bet that if he agreed to manage another mutual fund, investors would line up around the block to put their money forward. Different managers can also change the make-up of the fund's investments. If you do not agree with the new manager's investment strategy, switch funds.

How Much Money Do I Need?

Another appealing aspect of mutual funds it that you can still get a level of diversification without a lot of greenbacks. Each mutual fund will have a minimum investment to get started. Average minimum investments can range from $250 to $5,000, but there are funds for penny pinchers. An account can be opened at Twentieth Century with no money down as long as you agree to spend a $25 direct deposit each month. Just $25 per month gets you started in a mutual fund. Now who says investing is only for the well-to-do? Founders Funds, Invesco Funds Group, Janus Group, Neuberger & Berman Management, T. Rowe Price Associates, and Strong Funds also provide direct deposit programs, with no money down, for a $50 monthly investment. This is not an inclusive list, but it should give you confidence that there are mutual funds for your budget. Direct deposit investing each month allows the investor to benefit from dollar cost averaging, described in Investing's Tip #4.

Researching a Mutual Fund

Remember Investing's Tip #8 which states: never hand over money before first researching an investment. The following suggestions can help you compare and choose between funds.

First, you will remember from the beginning of this chapter that mutual funds are grouped by investment objective. If you know that you need a conservative investment for retirement, or if you are a risk averse person, or if you simply want to sleep better at night, "aggressive growth" mutual funds are not a good match for you. Concentrating on fund investment objectives that match your own will make your researching much easier and help limit the number of funds you need to investigate. In the end you will be much happier with your choice.

Second, you need to know and feel confident about the fund's investment holdings. Do not be fooled by thinking a particular fund contains all stocks, when in fact it could hold a percentage in precious metals. If you have been reading lately that precious metals are not performing as well as stocks or bonds, then maybe that fund is not right for you. Or if you are concerned about the future of the animal trapping industry, do not choose a fund with a majority holding in Beverly's Fine Furs and Mink Coats. Be sure the fund's investment holdings are in line with what you feel the future holds. A fund's investment holdings can be found in the **annual report**.

Third, do not forget to look at the fund's expense ratio, which can also be found in the annual report. This is not an expense to purchase shares in a fund. This separate expense measures how much investors pay for fund management. It is taken out before returns are given to investors. For example, 1.27% expense ratio means that $1.27 out of every $100 goes toward fund management. Compare similar mutual funds' expense ratios to each other in order to determine reasonableness.

The last suggestion is to analyze past returns. Most of us perform this step first, which is exactly why it is listed last. We get so excited with returns that we start at the top of a mutual fund list and run our fingers down the column of last year's return, highlighting the five largest returns. We then invest our money and at the end of the first quarter, our returns might be mediocre. Outraged, we yell, "How could this have happened?" Well, it happened because, as we know and you know too, nobody can accurately predict the future! Just because a mutual fund had above-average returns last year does not guarantee above-average returns this year. Mutual funds with above-average returns usually have above-average risk associated with them. You should not judge a mutual fund from only one year's worth of information. Go back to the first sentence; analyze returns*sssss*, meaning more than one. Look at a minimum of three to five years' worth of information. Because mutual fund investing styles go in and out of vogue, past returns offer no guarantee of future returns. However, determining an average rate of return over three or five years gives you a much better picture of the fund's average performance.

How Do I Calculate My Return On Investment?

It is easy to look up how a fund or other investment is performing, but what rate of return are you earning? First, specify a time period to analyze. You could compute a rate of return for a month, a quarter, a year, or any other time period. Simply subtract the total amount you paid for the investment from the total amount it is worth today. Add to that amount any interest, dividends (payments to you), or other money you received from the investment less all fees paid. Take that total amount and divide by the amount of your original investment. This will produce a percentage rate of return.

Mutual Funds - Are Fees a Factor?

When analyzing fund rates of return, you also need to consider fees. Generally, there are fees incurred when shares in a mutual fund are purchased. There are two terms that you will hear quite often, **load** and **no-load** funds. Loads are stated in percentages and are simply an up front fee to purchase shares in a mutual fund. For example, if you invest $2,500 in a mutual fund with a 5% load, then the fee to invest in that mutual fund will be $125 ($2,500 x 5%). No-load mutual funds are exactly how they sound, $0 in up front sales charges. This does not mean that no-load funds do not have additional fees. Other types of fees that can be incurred when purchasing a mutual fund are back-end loads, exit fees, and 12b-1 fees.

Back-end loads or **exit fees** are fees paid when you sell your shares rather than when you buy. A **12b-1 fee** is a marketing fee some funds charge each year. Up to 1.25% of the fund's assets can be used to pay for advertising and promotion. Even no-load funds can assess additional fees. Be sure to read the financial information thoroughly or ask directly to determine what fees can be incurred. It is important to understand the concept of fees and how they relate to your return.

If you paid the 5% load in the example above, you are initially investing $2,375 ($2,500 investment - $125 load fee). If a similar mutual fund with a 1% load ($2,475 initial investment) were yielding a 10% return, the 5% load fund would have to yield a 14.6% return for the two funds to be equal. This is quite possible. Take fees into consideration, along with your investment objectives, and base your decision on the expected rate of return.

Be Aware of Clone Funds

There are times when mutual funds close temporarily or permanently to outside investors. They continue to operate, but do not sell additional shares to new investors. Mutual funds can close when the fund manager decides that they have reached the maximum controllable amount. For example, a fund may close when the fund manager cannot find similar kinds of stocks which made the fund so successful. When a popular fund closes, often a new fund will open with a similar name. After Fidelity Equity Income fund closed to new investors, Fidelity created the Fidelity Equity Income II fund. Clone funds might overperform or underperform compared to the closed fund, but do not be mistaken by similar names or expect like returns. These funds may or may not have the same fund manager. They also might buy different securities which could make them two different kinds of funds.

Buying

Mutual funds can be purchased several ways. You can purchase shares directly from the mutual fund (they usually have toll-free numbers), or you can go through a brokerage firm or some banks. Each institution has some advantages. By purchasing shares directly from the fund, you skip the middleman. If you have more than one mutual fund, a brokerage firm or bank can consolidate your funds into one easy-to-read monthly account statement. In addition, some firms will let you switch in and out of funds for no extra charge.

You can set up the automatic investment plan through a brokerage firm, bank, or directly with the mutual fund you have chosen. Each month a specified amount will be transferred automatically (no checks to write). This way the money is set aside so you do not have to think about it or feel the pain. Most mutual fund management companies have toll-free telephone numbers which can be found by calling the toll-free directory at 1-800-555-1212.

Mutual Fund Mechanics

When you purchase a mutual fund you will buy shares of that fund at a stated price per share. Fund share prices are determined by the fund's net asset value divided by the number of shares. The **net asset value (NAV)** is determined by market value, which includes securities and cash, minus any financial obligations to other parties. You will keep the same number of shares over time unless you purchase more or the mutual fund pays a dividend and you elect to reinvest. Unless you need the money, we would recommend the reinvestment election. This means that any payments to you (dividends) will automatically be used to purchase more shares. This will accelerate accumulation of your money, and potentially avoid fees from investing that money at a later date.

The price per share of a mutual fund will change over time. You can track the price per share each weekday in *The Wall Street Journal* at the end of section "C," "Money & Investing." We chose the Fidelity Equity Income II Fund as our example. *The Wall Street Journal* lists the mutual fund's abbreviated name (EQII), the fund's objective or classification (EQI), the NAV per share ($19.02), the offer price per share which includes load fees (NL=No Load=$19.02), the change in NAV per share ($-0.05), and total return information stated in percentages (total return format changes daily). The offer price per share will be the same as the NAV per share with no-load (NL) mutual funds.

	Inv Obj.	NAV	Offer Price	NAV Chg.	Total Return		
					YTD	13 wks	3 yrs
Fidelity Invest:							
EQII	EQI	19.02	NL	-0.05	+17.3	+5.1	+30.1

Taxes

Taxes. How could we forget? Each mutual fund will be taxed differently depending upon its investments. For example, if your fund contains stocks that distribute dividends, you will have to pay tax on your share of the distributions. A statement showing your yearly taxable amounts will be sent to you. If you have questions on a specific mutual fund, ask the fund directly or consult a tax advisor or accountant.

The King Kongs of Mutual Funds

Listed below are 20 large and commonly referred to mutual fund companies. This does not mean that you don't have to research their funds nor does it mean that you should choose only from this list. It is simply a list to familiarize yourself with common mutual fund company names.

Mutual Fund Companies

Fidelity

Investment Company of America

Washington Mutual Investors

Windsor

Vanguard

Income Fund of America

Janus

Aim Weingarten

Wellington

Dreyfus

Twentieth Century

Dean Witter

Merrill Lynch

American

Kemper

Painewebber

Prudential

Shearson

Growth Fund of America

Pioneer

Types of Mutual Funds

This section might be difficult to read straight through and will be best used as a reference tool. Highlight categories of interest and research funds within that classification. You will find that different financial publications will group mutual funds into slightly different categories. This is because they use slightly different criteria for classification. The mutual fund categories listed are arranged in order from high risk to conservative. For the fund categories that fall in the middle, it is difficult to assign an overall risk classification. It is also sometimes difficult to assign one risk classification to a group of mutual funds, because the best determinant of risk is an analysis of the securities held in each mutual fund.

Risk is often determined by **beta.** Beta is used to measure the risk of equity mutual funds, simply because equity mutual funds contain a portion of their assets in stocks. One of the most common measures of risk for a particular company is its beta. Beta measures the risk of a stock compared against the market average. The market beta always equals 1.0. Funds with a beta higher than 1.0 are considered more risky than the market average. For example an equity mutual fund with a beta of 1.1 is expected to perform 10% better than the market in an up market and 10% worse in a down market. Don't be left guessing. Remember that beta greater than 1.0 means greater risk.

The best way to determine risk and ratings is by looking up a particular mutual fund through the following resources: *Morningstar Mutual Funds*, *Charles Schwab Mutual Funds Performance Guide*, *Business Week*'s "Mutual Fund Scoreboard," and *Money*'s monthly mutual fund ratings. There is also *Morningstar 5 Star Investor*, which is a monthly publication that includes fund news and ratings. These resources analyze mutual funds and assign a level of risk based upon their findings. Remember, you can reduce overall risk by investing for the long-term.

The following 21 investment objective categories will help identify specific groups of mutual funds that are best suited to your personal investment goals and desired level of risk. These are general categories that are not all inclusive or definitive. They are meant to give you an idea of what exists and to help get you started. Risk will vary within each category.

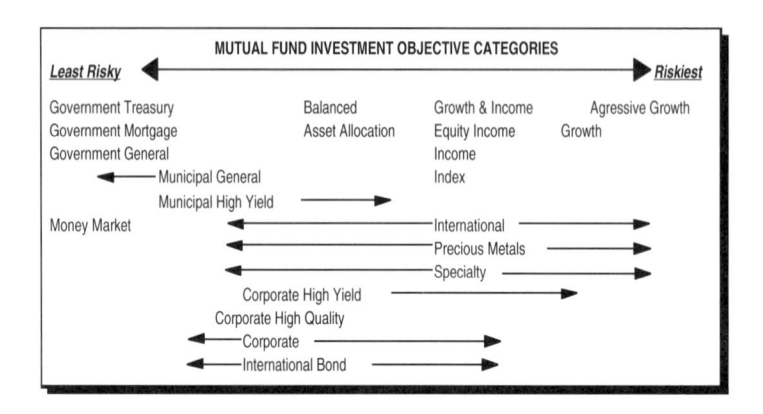

Aggressive Growth Funds

Objective - maximize capital gains through aggressive investment strategies. They usually invest in small, emerging growth stocks that do not pay dividends. The portfolios of these funds tend toward the "hot" industries such as computer software or biotechnology. There is high potential for return, but on the other hand there is a high level of risk.

Risk - high. Mutual funds in this category are not meant for conservative uses. So if you are risk-averse or are choosing a mutual fund for a retirement account, you will want to look elsewhere. If you want the risk, they can be appropriate for a small percentage of your portfolio.

Growth Funds

Objective - long-term capital growth. They generally do not engage in speculative tactics (complex stock trading). They differ from aggressive growth funds by tending to invest in older and larger growth-oriented firms. As in aggressive growth, dividends are nil or small.

It is important to understand that growth funds can be one of two types: growth stock funds or value funds.

Growth stock funds buy into companies that have strong earnings growth, a dominant presence in their markets, and do not rely on economic cycles to turn a profit. Value funds are also growth funds, but they attempt to purchase cyclical stocks at the bottom of their economic cycle. These stocks may include auto makers, steel manufacturers, home builders and banks. These are two different strategies for growth mutual fund managers. One is not more correct than the other, but it is important to know the distinction so you will make an educated choice.

Risk - lower risk than aggressive growth funds. This is the largest category of equity funds so you will probably see the name over and over. Growth mutual funds can produce the same returns as aggressive funds except it may take longer.

Growth and Income Funds

Objective - long-term capital growth and income generation. They generally invest in stocks of established companies (blue chip stocks) which pay cash dividends.

Risk - falls in the middle between risky and conservative. Mutual fund companies often recommend this category for retirement accounts.

Equity-Income Funds

Objective - high level of income generation. Generally consists of dividend-paying stocks and bonds.

Risk - also falls in the middle. Depending upon the mutual fund, it could be more or less risky than a growth and income fund.

Income Funds

Objective - high level of income generation. Similar to equity-income funds which consist of dividend-paying stocks and bonds. The difference is that they can devote a greater portion of their assets to bonds and money market funds.

Risk - because income funds can devote a greater portion of their assets to more liquid investments, they can potentially have lower risk than equity-income funds.

Index Funds

Objective - provide investment returns that attempt to match an index, such as the Standard & Poor's index of 500 stocks. Explained in Chapter 5, this is a compiled return of 500 stocks.

Risk - index funds can carry about the same amount of risk as a growth and income fund.

Balanced Funds

Objective - preserve original investment while providing current income and long-term growth.

Risk - balanced funds are one of the lower-risk mutual fund categories. This is a sensible fund category for a conservative investment.

Asset Allocation Funds

Objective - similar to balanced funds. The difference is they choose the balance between investment holdings.

International Funds

Objective - invest exclusively in foreign securities. Global funds are sometimes grouped in this classification. The difference being that global funds can invest in foreign, as well as U.S., securities. Each mutual fund in this category will invest differently. Some have portfolios in individual countries, others in several countries combined.

Risk - it is difficult to determine a level of risk for international funds. International funds may be a good way to diversify your portfolio; however, there are times when the U.S. economy is performing more strongly than those of foreign countries. In general, these funds carry a higher degree of risk, especially those that invest exclusively in foreign securities. Pay attention to global economic news if you hold mutual funds in this category.

Precious Metals Funds

Objective - long-term capital growth through investment in gold, silver, and other precious metals, as well as the stocks of mining companies.

Risk - low to high, can be volatile during short periods.

Specialty Funds

Objective - limits investments to a specific industry or economic sector such as technology or health care.

Risk - the narrower the fund's industry or economic sector, the less diversification provided, and generally the riskier the fund.

Bond Funds:

Corporate High-Yield Funds

Objective - invest in high-yield corporate bond funds or what are otherwise known as **junk bonds** (bonds with low quality rating).

Risk - low to high risk. Bond funds in general have lower risk than equity funds, but high-yield funds could be riskier.

Corporate High-Quality Funds

Objective - generate income by investing in all types of bonds. These funds can be grouped into short/intermediate and long-term bond maturity lengths. Portfolios of short/intermediate funds hold bonds which will usually mature in ten years or less, as opposed to long-term funds containing bonds which take over ten years to mature. Many corporate bond funds contain U.S. government bonds in order to keep a high rating and make the fund less risky.

Risk - can be lower risk than corporate high-yield fund. Primarily holds bonds that have a strong capacity to pay interest and principal, but are more susceptible to changing economic climates.

Corporate - General Funds

Objective - generate income by investing primarily in corporate bonds. These funds can also be grouped into short/intermediate and long-term bond maturity lengths.

Risk - low to high. Each fund will hold a different portfolio of bonds rated from the highest quality down to junk bonds. Be sure to read the financial information to determine the amount of risk involved.

International Bond Funds

Objective - generate income by investing in debt securities of foreign companies. If the fund is included within the global category, then part of the portfolio can contain U.S. securities, as well as foreign.

Risk - same risk factor applies to international bond funds as international funds, except that any type of debt (bond) security usually carries less risk than an equity (stock) security.

Municipal High Yield Funds

Objective - generate income by purchasing lower-rated or non-rated tax-free bonds; in other words, junk municipal bonds. Income that is generated is exempt from federal income tax.

Risk - more risky than municipal bond funds since the portfolio contains lower-rated bonds that have a higher possibility of default.

Municipal General Funds (Short/Intermediate and Long-Term)

Objective - generate income by investing in municipal securities issued by state and local governments. Income that is generated is exempt from federal income tax, and in some instances state and local tax as well. For example, if you live in California and buy shares of a mutual fund that invests solely in California municipal bonds (single state fund), the income earned is exempt from federal and state taxes.

Risk - not risk-free, especially single state funds. There have been instances where state or local governments have defaulted on municipal bonds. For greater security, choose a fund that invests in several different states. Remember to take into account the tax savings from municipal funds when comparing their rates of return to other funds.

Government Mortgage Funds

Objective - generate income and maintain original investment by mainly purchasing **mortgage-backed securities** such as Federal National Mortgage Association (Fannie Mae), Government National Mortgage Association (Ginnie Mae), and Federal Home Loan Mortgage Corporation (Freddie Mac).

Risk - carry slightly more risk than government treasury funds listed below, even though principal and interest is guaranteed by the federal agencies listed above. They usually offer slightly higher rates of return compared to government treasury funds.

Government General Funds

Objective - generate income and maintain original investment by purchasing securities backed by the U.S. government and its agencies. Funds in this category can also be short/intermediate or long-term maturity lengths. Risk - low risk because all securities held in the portfolio are backed by the U.S. government and its agencies. Do not be fooled that all funds in this category are the same. The different blend of securities contained in each portfolio can produce different rates of return.

Government Treasury Funds

Objective - generate income and maintain original investment by purchasing U.S. government securities. These funds can also be grouped into short/intermediate and long-term funds.

Risk - virtually risk-free because your investment is backed by the federal government.

Money Market Funds

Objective - generate income and maintain original investment by purchasing safe, short-term securities. Money market funds act similarly to a bank savings account and are just as liquid an investment. The market value is usually maintained at a constant $1 per share.

Risk - one of the safest investments that can be found. Some people use money market funds in place of a savings account. Money market funds will usually offer slightly higher interest rates than a savings account and many come with check writing capabilities. They do carry a higher degree of risk than an insured savings account.

In summary, take the time to research mutual funds. They can provide you with diversification and a desired level of risk, with little money down. Mutual funds are a great place to start investing. Do not be intimidated by the volume of funds. Need more help? Look up *How to*

Select Top-Performing Mutual Fund Investments (International Informational Associates), by Aaron H. Coleman and David H. Coleman; *The Handbook for No-Load Fund Investors* (No-Load Investor Inc.), by Sheldon Jacobs and *The Fidelity Guide to Mutual Funds: A Complete Guide to Investing in Mutual Funds* (Fireside, Simon & Schuster), by Mary Bowland.

CHAPTER 5

STOCKS

The first thing that comes to mind when people think of **stocks** is Wall Street and the New York Stock Exchange. However, there is a lot more to stocks than just the frantic buying and selling that we see in movies. The concept of buying and selling stocks started in May 1792, when twenty-four men met every morning to buy and sell securities for themselves and their friends under a buttonwood tree. In 1793, they decided that they needed their morning coffee, and moved to the Tontine Coffee House at the corner of William Street and Wall. In 1817, the New York and Stock Exchange Board, as it was then called, was created. As Ellen Williamson put it so well, "Zoologically it is where the bulls and the bears prey like wolves on sheep; theoretically it is the home plate of the financial world; figuratively it is Big Business anywhere; and realistically it is where a huge auction goes on each day between people who have securities to buy and sell."

Today, stocks can be traded in several different places in addition to the **New York Stock Exchange (NYSE)**. Popular arenas include the **American Stock Exchange (AMEX)** and **NASDAQ (National Association of Securities Dealers Automated Quotations)**, which is a computerized trading system for **Over-the-Counter (OTC)** stocks. Stocks traded on the NASDAQ are usually smaller and newer companies.

Trading in the stock market can be one of the most intimidating activities for an amateur investor, but it can also reap the greatest benefits. Often, amateur investors are guided away from the stock market, but stocks can complement the portfolio of any eager amateur investor. Over the last 70 years, stocks have out-performed all other investments. Stocks provide various levels of risk from conservative to risky. They will take more time to manage than mutual funds, but can reap greater rewards and be fun to follow.

When investing in the stock market, it is important not to panic and get scared out of your stocks. Investing in stocks should be performed for the long-term. If you're saying to yourself, "I don't have to understand the stock market because I'm investing all of my loot in a mutual fund," think again. It is very possible that the mutual fund you choose has stock investments, so you will want to understand how the stock market works. This chapter will start you walking in the shallow end of the pool with "How To Get Started" and "How To Buy Stocks," and eventually will teach you how to swim in the deep end with "$tock Price" analysis.

How to Get Started

Like any investment, stocks need to be researched, but how do you know which companies to begin researching? Simple, keep your eyes and ears open! For example, if there's a local company with great products and/or service, find out if it's public and then look into it. *Value Line Investment Survey* or *Standard & Poor's* are excellent sources of financial information on specific companies. *Value Line* also publishes *The Outlook* report. It is only a couple of pages (for those with limited time), but contains valuable information on economic data and stock highlights.

Remember Investing's Tip #7, read financial publications, even if it takes a while to get used to. Reading any of the publications listed will provide you with an abundance of companies to consider. Pick out the companies that interest you or the companies whose products and services are familiar to you.

Emerging companies in your area or products that seem to sell exceptionally well could be a good lead. What company makes these products? Is that a public company? In what stores or on what products do you spend your money? That guilty feeling you get after Liz Claiborne shopping binges or the enormous phone bills from AT&T might be relieved by investing in those companies if they meet your criteria. Next time a spending impulse occurs, you can think of it as benefiting your investment!

As you read through magazines or if you own shares in mutual funds, take a look at what companies the mutual fund managers are investing in for their funds. This is a great resource for one simple reason. Observing mutual fund managers' investment choices provides you with free advice from a financial professional who manages a large sum of money for a living. This should spark ideas. You still need to do your own research because by the time you read it, the fund manager might have already sold.

Take suggestions from friends and colleagues, but be sure to do your own research. Don't rely on your best friend's stock pick until you have seen the proof. We want to recommend some additional literature about buying and selling stocks, but where do we begin? At your local bookstore and library are enough books about the stock market to choke on. We enjoy Peter Lynch's writing style in *One up on Wall Street* (Penguin Books) and *Beating the Street* (Simon & Schuster), but there are an abundance of other stock market books available. Enjoy!!

Opening an Account & Selecting a Broker

Opening an account is a relatively simple process. It falls well below the agony level of buying a new washing machine or a new car. Step one: break apart the piggy bank.

An account can be opened at either a **discount brokerage firm** such as Charles Schwab or a **full service brokerage firm** such as Merrill Lynch. Both full service and discount brokerage firms will buy and sell securities, but a full service brokerage firm will also give investment and financial planning advice. If you feel you need the additional investment and financial planning advice, you may want to do business through a full service brokerage firm. You will generally pay more for the full service because of the additional services you receive. Ask around for some good recommendations of stockbrokers, rather than just calling a brokerage firm out of the blue. The brokers who are always available to take your call are possibly available for a specific reason — investors do not want to do business with them. Choose someone who is willing to work within your investment objectives and who will give you the attention you deserve. Remember, investing is not just for the wealthy. If your stockbroker does not pay full attention to your account, no matter how small, you have the power to fire him or her!

Full service brokerage firms can assist investors in determining what investments suit their needs, such as a retirement fund. Brokers may give excellent advice, but it is still important to do your own research. Do not invest blindly. We were not so lucky in the beginning. Feeling confident about our knowledge, we chose from the start to invest through a discount brokerage firm. After investing for quite a while, we came down with the doubter's blues. Were we missing something by not using a full service brokerage firm? Our rate of return was high through the discount broker, but could we do better?

A friend of ours sensed our concern and recommended a friend of his who just happened to be a stockbroker. We called him the next day, and lo and behold, he had just received word of a "hot stock tip." We were so pleased with ourselves that we bought the stock the minute the market opened the next day. Since this book went to press, that "hot stock" has continued to fall further and further. They say that the middle of the earth is a fiery pit, so maybe that is what he meant by "hot stock."

We have only ourselves to blame because we did not do our homework and research this company thoroughly. We should have caught on when we called him one afternoon, a little upset over the stock price, and he told us there was still time for the stock to rebound because the market had not closed yet. This was 3:00 in the afternoon on the west coast. He knew that the market closed at 4:00 p.m., but had not figured out the time difference. Here's a helpful tip: the New York Stock Exchange is open from 9:30 a.m. until 4:00 p.m. Eastern Standard Time! This story does have a happy ending because after that experience we have done business with very intelligent stockbrokers and financial planners, so do not give up hope. However, we always research the companies no matter how competent our brokers are.

If you begin doing your own research and feel confident with your investing abilities, you may want to open an account with a discount brokerage firm. The greatest advantage of a discount broker is the money you save on transaction fees. Using a full service brokerage firm can cost more than twice as much, depending on the transaction size. However, this is not always the case. Be sure to ask both discount and full service brokers about their fee structures.

Some people get upset at the high fees and ask why these firms have to charge fees at all. It's simple: this is the way they make money. Just like you and me, they have to eat and provide shelter for themselves. Of course, their shelters might be much grander than ours, but this is their business. Would you open a cookie store and only sell cookies at cost? Of course not. You would include a profit for yourself. Now let's turn the situation around. If you were a consumer at this cookie store, would you buy the exact same oatmeal raisin cookie for $.60 or $.90? A reasonable consumer would choose the $.60 cookie, unless the owner went out of his way to sprinkle white chocolate chunks on top of the cookie. If this happens to please you immensely, you would buy the $.90 cookie. This is the same principle for choosing a brokerage firm. If all you want to do is trade securities, then choose the $.60 discounted cookie, but if you want more, choose the full service $.90 cookie.

How a Stock is Born

The stock market is a constantly changing environment. New stocks are continually being born and brought to the market. They arrive at the market, wrapped in ticker tape, carried by a giant stork . . . sorry, wrong story. New stocks appear in the form of an **Initial Public Offering (IPO)**. New companies give up a share of their ownership and issue stock. A **prospectus** will be prepared on the new firm and given away to interested investors. An investor purchases the shares of stock before its first day of trading. IPOs have the stereotype of reaping huge rewards, so many are hard to acquire unless you are a preferred customer at a brokerage house. (We will put this in simple terms: Preferred customer = lots of $,$$$,$$$s.) However, there are IPOs that do not get much attention. Remember to ask yourself why they have not received attention. It could be because nobody wants the stock. Therefore, if you are small investor without much money, be wary of IPO shares offered to you. IPOs are very exciting to watch, but again they require a high degree of effort and thorough research. This is not for the faint-hearted.

The Stock Section for the Faint-hearted

This next section is written specifically for the faint-hearted. We know there are discouraged people reading this chapter saying "I know I'm faint-hearted, but I want to invest in stocks!" You're in luck. There are less risky stocks (not riskless, but less risky) called **blue chip stocks**. Blue chip stocks are those of stable, well established companies, with solid historical rates of return and high prospects for long term growth. For example, Walt Disney and Coca-Cola are considered blue chip stocks. For the past 10 years, Walt Disney's and Coca-Cola's dividends and stock prices have steadily increased each year. Do not sink into your recliner chair too far because blue chip stocks of today may not always perform as well as in past years. Remember, it is just as important to do your homework with blue chips as with other companies.

Here is another helpful reminder for the faint-hearted. One of the most common measures of risk, as stated in the mutual fund chapter, is beta. Beta is used to measure the risk of a stock compared against the market average. Since the term "beta" has already been discussed, we will ask the questions this time. Question: What is the market beta? Answer: 1.0. Question: How is stock with a 1.2 beta expected to perform? Answer: 20% better than the market in an up market and 20% worse in a down market. Betas of different companies can be found in *Value Line Investment Survey* and *Standard & Poor's Stock Reports*.

The Never-Ending Big "D" - Diversification

When you read about stocks, you see the word "diversification." We briefly mentioned diversification in Investing's Tip #2, but let's expand on that point. Diversification, simply stated, means spreading investments around to minimize risk in a portfolio. A portfolio, you remember, is another word for the collection of your investments, whether they are stocks, bonds, mutual funds, IRAs, cash or a combination of all five. Investors love to hear the phrase "minimize risk," because all investing requires some degree of risk and anything that can reduce it is welcomed with open arms. Do not be single minded and invest only in pharmaceutical or heavy construction equipment companies. Spread the wealth among several different industries. There could come a time when pharmaceutical companies have government-controlled profits or new construction is well below average. A diversified portfolio will offset industry slumps and give you better performance.

If you are only investing in stocks, how many are needed to make up a diversified stock portfolio? The standard range is from five to 15 stocks. A general rule of thumb in owning stocks is to never hold more than you can handle. By now, you should have a strong feeling that buying and holding stocks requires effort on the investor's part. An investor should only hold as many stocks as he/she is willing to exert the energy to manage. Think of this as standing in a batting cage hitting baseballs. When the balls are pitched slowly with long intervals between each pitch, the amateur batter has time to set up and has the potential to hit a home run each time. But if more balls are pitched at a faster rate, the amateur batter has less time to set up, ending up with a couple of doubles and striking out more often. Nobody wants to strike out on an investment, so only hold as many stocks as you have the time to watch.

Stock Indexes

"The Dow Jones is currently up eight points." "The Dow Jones fell five points today to close at 3,325." Does either of the last two sentences sound familiar? If you listen to the radio or television, you cannot help hearing about the **Dow Jones Industrial Average (DJIA)**, but what exactly does it mean? The Dow Jones Industrial Average is the most popular barometer of the stock market. It currently consists of the following 30 stocks.

Dow Jones Industrial Average

Alliedsignal	IBM
Alcoa	International Paper
American Express	J.P. Morgan
AT&T	McDonald's
Bethlehem Steel	Merck
Boeing	3M
Caterpillar	Phillip Morris
Chevron	Procter & Gamble
Coca-Cola	Sears Roebuck
Du Pont	Texaco
Eastman Kodak	Union Carbide
Exxon	United Technologies
General Electric	Walt Disney
General Motors	Westinghouse
Goodyear	Woolworth

Whenever one of these 30 stocks fall or rise in price, the Dow Jones Industrial Average is affected. Does this mean that if the Dow Jones is down ten points for the day, that your stock is also down in price? No. The combined closing stock price of the companies listed in the Dow Jones will be down ten points, but a single company's stock could be up for the day.

Other stock indexes are the **Russell 2000**, which is an index of small stocks, and the **S&P 500**. The S&P 500 is an index of 500 stocks, which represents approximately 75% of the total capital of the United States stock market. It includes actively traded stocks in 87 industries. Many investors use the S&P 500 as a base for assessing financial performance.

How to Read a Stock Market Page from a Newspaper

Any large newspaper should contain stock quotes, but the best source of stock and market quotes is *The Wall Street Journal*. Stock quotes will be listed by exchange. We chose Microsoft for the example listed on the next page. *The Wall Street Journal* lists a stock's high and low price for the past 52 weeks ($98, $70.38) It then lists the company name (Microsoft), ticker symbol (MSFT, abbreviated company name), regular annual dividend paid (no dividend paid), yield on the annual dividend (dividend ÷ current price), the company's P/E ratio (25, explained later in the chapter), and the number of shares sold for the day (2,856,000). The last few columns report the stock price for the day. The high and low price paid per share ($84, $79.50), followed by the closing price ($80.25) and net change from yesterday (+$1.75). If there are no dividend amounts listed, the company does not

52 Weeks		Stock	Sym	Div	Yld %	PE	Vol 100's	Hi	Lo	Close	Net Chg
Hi	Low										
60 3/8	43	AnheuserB	BUD	1.44f	3.0	14	6255	48 7/8	48 3/8	48 3/8	+ 3/8
30	17 1/2	AnnTaylor	ANN		- - -	- - -	506	28 1/4	27 5/8	28 1/8	+ 1/2
63 3/8	46 3/4	BellSouth	BLS	2.76	4.4	20	5921	63	61 1/2	62 3/8	+ 1/2
98	**70 3/8**	**Microsoft**	**MSFT**		**- - -**	**25**	**28560**	**84**	**79 1/2**	**80 1/4**	**+1 3/4**
47 7/8	35 3/8	Disney	DIS	0.25	0.6	24	18384	43 3/4	42 1/8	42 3/8	- 7/8
s74 1/4	31 1/4	Intel	INTC	.20	0.3	13	52225	63 3/4	61 7/8	62 1/4	- 3/4
s28 1/4	14	Starbucks	SBUX		- - -	cc	2016	27 1/4	25 3/4	26	- 1/4

give a dividend.

With NASDAQ issues, you might see a **bid** and **asked** price. The bid price is the price interested investors are willing to pay for a share of stock. The asked price is the price at which current holders of the stock are willing to sell their shares. The difference between the bid and asked price is referred to as the **spread**.

How To Buy Stocks

After your account is opened and you have decided on the stocks you want to purchase, the transaction is only a phone call away. On the phone you can order a specific number of shares at a specific price. You can attempt to buy stocks at any price you choose, similar to how an auction works. However, like an auction, if your bid is too low you will not buy the stock at that price. Requesting to buy stock at the **market value** is a guaranteed purchase. Your order will be placed and the purchase price will be the stock's selling price at the time your order was executed. You can also specify the maximum price at which you would be willing to buy a particular stock. For example, if you have been watching Anheuser Busch move around $50 per share, but have a feeling that it will fall to $47 per share within the next week, then you can place a **limit order** to buy a specified amount of shares at $47 per share. If at any time during trading the stock falls to $47 per share, your order will be activated and you will be the owner of shares in Anheuser Busch. You can place your limit order as **good until canceled** which keeps your order open and active until you cancel. This process also works for selling a stock. You can place a **stop order** if you know that you would want to sell the stock if it fell to a specified price per share.

When buying stocks, you might hear the terms **round** versus **odd lots**. Purchasing less than 100 shares of a company is considered an odd lot. Round lots are sold in multiples of 100 shares. Do not think you have to save enough to purchase a round lot. Many of our purchases are in odd lots. Be sure to ask a brokerage firm about round versus odd lot purchases, as some brokerage firms may charge more for purchasing odd lots.

Buying On Margin

Most brokerage firms will also let you buy stock on **margin**. They may speak of margins in casual terms, but you do not want to get involved in margins until you are confident in your abilities in the stock market. Even then, this might not be a good idea. Buying on margin is similar to taking out a loan to buy stocks and securities. Firms will loan you a specified percentage of your portfolio value which can be used to purchase securities. You pay interest on the loan amount, but do not have to pay back the balance as long as your portfolio value keeps rising or remains constant. However, if your portfolio value falls below the specified percentage level, you will get a *dreaded* margin call and be asked to deposit more money into your account or sell current securities (potentially at a loss) to maintain the specified ratio of borrowed to portfolio value. If you are going to buy on margin, do not overextend yourself. *Make sure you have access to money in case you get a margin call.*

Watching a Stock and Knowing When to Sell

Once you are the proud new parent of a stock, you will

probably do what every new parent does — watch your stock every minute of the day. It will not take long to find free stock quote services in your city and become addicted to calling every hour. One day, you'll find out your stock is up a point and in an elated voice you scream "I made a point!" Wait a minute, what does a point mean? Simple, a point is equal to $1. If you owned 100 shares and your stock went up 1 point, that would equal $100. Although it is hard to resist, try not to hover over your stocks, because you do not want to get unduly scared and sell. Stock prices will fall and rise even for the best of companies. It is important to ride out these fluctuations unless there is a *reason to sell*. Do not worry about your over enthusiastic addiction in the beginning. It took us about six months to come down to a level of only calling for stock quotes once a day.

When buying stocks, you should always have a plan for when to sell. First, consider why you bought the stock in the first place. Let's say you bought stock in a company in anticipation of a hot new product. If that product turns out to be a consumer nightmare, you should immediately consider selling. What if you bought stock for capital growth and noticed earnings were steadily decreasing each quarter? Perhaps you then did your research and found this decrease was due to increasing administrative costs. It appears this company has a hard time controlling costs. This may be another good reason to consider selling.

Second, forget about what price you paid for the stock and analyze the stock's current price to what you feel is the expected or future price. If the premise you based your original purchase decision upon has not changed, then hold on. If you feel the stock's future price will be lower, sell. Do not be stubborn or become psychologically attached.

You can also set a limit for gains and losses on each of your stocks stated in a percentage. For example, you could decide that if the stock price gains or falls by 15%, you will re-evaluate the company and decide if selling would be best. Do not let the thought of paying taxes on gains inhibit your decision to sell.

Taxes

The government takes a great interest in your stock investments. They will not hold your hand and help you with your decisions, but rest assured the I.R.S. wants to hear about your great money-making stocks. We are not tax specialists, and would encourage you to ask a tax advisor or accountant for advice, however the following section is a summary of basic federal tax laws. Do not forget about individual state taxes, even though we do not summarize them here.

You can hold onto a stock and never pay a penny of taxes as long as you do not sell any shares or receive any dividends. Once you sell shares of a stock, you will be taxed on the capital gain or you can deduct the capital loss against other capital gains. Capital gains or losses refer to the difference between the price you bought the stock and the price at which you sold. Short-term capital gains are taxed at your federal income tax rate. They occur when shares are held less than one year and are sold. Long-term capital gains are taxed at your federal income tax rate up to 28%. Long-term gains occur when shares are sold after more than one year and one day. If your income tax rate is 31% or higher, there are advantages to only realize long-term gains. On the other hand, if your income tax rate is 28% or lower, there is no difference in taxes between short-term and long-term gains. If you lose money on a sale of a stock, you can deduct the net capital losses (capital losses less capital gains) against ordinary income up to $3,000 annually. Any excess losses over $3,000 can be carried forward to the next year. For example, suppose that in one year you realize losses of $500 on the sale of XYZ stock and gains of $400 on the sale of ABC stock. Add capital gains of $400 to capital losses of ($500) which equals ($100). This $100 capital loss can be deducted against ordinary income. Capital losses can also be offset against other realized capital gains on investments such as art or real estate.

It is common for an investor to purchase shares of a stock at different times and at different share prices. How do you determine the capital gain or loss if only a portion of the shares are sold? The investor can designate on the tax return which shares are being sold at their original purchase price.

December is a busy month for stock investors, and it is not because of last-minute Christmas shopping. December is the last month of the tax year for individuals. It is the time when investors sell losing stocks to offset gains taken on winning stocks for tax purposes. It does not take long to devise a plan to sell stocks on December 31 at a loss in value, offset this loss against stock gains incurred throughout the year, then buy back the same stock on January 1 of the new year. If this were the case, one could realistically never pay taxes on gains realized from stock sold. However, the government has a plan of their own called the wash-sale rule. The wash-sale rule occurs when an investor sells a security at a loss, then purchases securities that are substantially identical to those sold within a 61 day period. This rule only applies to losses. It covers 30 days before the sale and ends 30 days afterward. If the sale of your stock falls under these circumstances, a tax deduction is disallowed for losses.

For more information on how to defer capital gains or additional questions on security tax laws, contact a tax advisor or accountant.

Common vs. Preferred Stock

There are actually two kinds of stocks, common and preferred. **Common stocks** can pay a dividend and grant voting privileges. Throughout the text, when we refer to a "stock," it is common stock. **Preferred stocks** carry fixed dividends that must be paid to the investor before common stock dividends are paid. Preferreds are not traded heavily, so generally when people talk about stocks, they are referring to common stocks.

$tock Price

At the beginning of this chapter, we said that we would begin in the shallow end and eventually let you swim in the deep end of the pool. Discussing stock price can get technical because it introduces unfamiliar terms. This next section is designed to provide you with several tools to use in determining a stock's price or worth. Do not be frustrated if these tools sound like a foreign language. Use this section as a reference. You will hear these terms mentioned often by brokers, financial analysts, in magazine articles, and on television.

A stock is valued and priced at whatever the market says it is worth. The market will adjust the price of a stock by buying and selling shares. Who influences the market? Why, investors, of course. What influences investors? Unfortunately, everything does; that is the sole reason playing the stock market is not an exact science! The day *The Wall Street Journal* publishes on the front page, "Disney To Quit Animation Business: All resources will be directed towards widget manufacturing," will probably be the day that Disney's stock price will fall through the floor. The drop in value will not be caused by a poor financial statement or a low price-to-earnings ratio, but rather by investors' expectations that Disney's future profits will decline because of the lack of expertise in widget manufacturing. If playing the stock market was an exact science, we could enter several exact calculations into a computer and derive a stock's value. What a perfect world that would be. Besides investors' own emotions, interest rates, political developments, Wall Street gossip, and company promotional hype, there are several financial guides investors use to determine a stock's worth.

1) Earnings per Share (EPS). EPS = (Net income minus preferred stock dividends) ÷ average number of **common shares outstanding**. Simply stated, it is the amount of earnings attributable to each share of stock. EPS is a key statistic in evaluating a stock's potential outlook. Analysts will usually try to predict a company's earnings, on a quarterly basis. Investors want to see earnings per share increasing over time for any company. This sends a message to the public that the company is either growing or performing more efficiently.

2) Price to Earnings Ratio (P/E). P/E Ratio = current price of stock ÷ earnings per share (defined above). This ratio reflects market expectations for a stock. For example, a P/E ratio of 10 means that investors are willing to pay 10 times earnings for a share of that stock. It is not possible for us to discuss P/E ratios to their full extent within the scope of this book, but we do want to define it and make you aware that it can have several different meanings.

There are two schools of thought in analyzing P/E ratios. On one hand, stocks with a high P/E ratio can suggest that investors perceive the company to have a strong potential for greater earnings. However, stocks with high P/E ratios can also be considered riskier investments because there is a possibility that higher earnings will never be realized. On the other hand, stocks with low P/E ratios can be considered undervalued. If investors do not have confidence in the earnings potential of a company, there is a chance that this will affect the stock price.

How do you know what is considered a high or low ratio? For instance, a stock in one industry could have a P/E ratio of 10 and a stock in a different industry have a P/E ratio of 25. They could both be considered "average" in the market. Why? Because each industry will have an average P/E ratio to compare against. Industries such as public utilities, customarily have low P/E ratios, while others, such as software, normally have higher P/E ratios. For the P/E ratio to be useful, it must be compared to the P/E ratio of other companies in the same industry. Remember, playing the stock market is not an exact science and each company needs to be examined individually. Helpful hint: P/E ratio information on specific companies can be found in *Value Line Investment Survey* and *Standard & Poor's Stock Reports.*

3) Book Value per Share. Book value per share = **stockholders' equity** ÷ number of common shares outstanding. This is another tool to judge if a stock is overvalued. If a company's stock price is lower than its book value per share, it can be considered a bargain. This conclusion is true as long as the stock price is not being held low by a company's impending financial problems.

4) Size of Dividend. A dividend is a payment made to each shareholder on a per share basis. For example, if Coca Cola gave $.56 per share in dividends and you owned 100 shares, you would have received $56. Think of it as your share of the profits earned. Not all companies give dividends to their shareholders. These companies take the profit and reinvest it back into the company for further growth. For example, Lotus traditionally does not give dividends, but uses part of the profits for research and development efforts. Whether or not a company pays dividends does not determine if its share price has growth potential. Stocks that give dividends can have growth potential as well. For companies that do pay dividends, annual increases in the dividend are usually a good sign. If dividends are decreasing each year, investors may not feel confident about the company's financial health and sell the stock.

We have just described ways to evaluate a stock's worth, but how do you evaluate a company's worth? Someone told us, "Don't worry about the numbers; it's a great company." We chose not to do business with this individual. The numbers are important because they can potentially save you from investing in a company that will be bankrupt in six months. The best way to make your decision is to choose companies that are in solid financial positions. In the next chapter, titled "Annual Reports & Prospectuses," you will learn how to choose companies with a clean bill of financial health.

Heavy Duty Stock Trading

The next three sections contain information on heavy duty buying and selling of stock using advanced trading strategies. These strategies are used by professional full-time stock watchers and should not be attempted by stock gazers. Not until you feel extremely comfortable trading stocks, if even then, should you attempt these next three strategies. One might make an analogy of the novice stock trader playing the options game to an unexperienced river rafter paddling white water rapids. Both are likely to lead to disaster. We do not expect you to start trading options, but a chapter on stocks would be incomplete without at least mentioning these strategies. Someday, you might be an expert and want to try these types of trading. But for now, we want you to know what they are and the high degree of risk associated with them. This will keep you from being pushed into this arena unknowingly.

Selling Short

When you **sell a stock short**, you are anticipating that the stock will fall in price. For example, suppose a stock is at $50 per share and you place a short sale for 100 shares. You can think of it as borrowing 100 shares from the broker. If the price falls to $40 per share, you would buy the 100 shares at $40 per share to replace the borrowed shares, and gain $10 per share. On the other hand, if the price rises to $60 per share, you have to buy the 100 shares at $60 to replace the borrowed shares. This represents a loss of $10 per share. Selling short has a high degree of risk because the stock price could rise dramatically.

Put and Call Options

An **option contract** gives the investor the right to buy (**call**) or sell (**put**) a security at a specified price (**exercise** or **strike price**) within a specified amount of time. Put and call options are bought at a premium which is determined mainly by the relationship between the exercise price and the market price of the stock, by the volatility of the stock, and by the time remaining on the contract before the expiration date. For example, suppose a stock is selling for $40 per share and you think it is going to rise to $60 per share within two months. You can buy one call option to purchase 100 shares of the stock at $40 per share in two months. Let's say the option premium costs $500. One option equals the right to buy/sell 100 shares. A quote price in *The Wall Street Journal* of $5 for a December 40 is equal to $500 ($5 x 100). At the end of two months your speculation was correct and the stock has risen to $60 per share. You can exercise the option at $40 per share which will cost you $4,000 ($40 x 100 shares), and immediately sell the stock for $60 per share or $6,000. Your total profit would equal $1,500 ($6,000 - $4,000 - $500 = $1,500). Also, since the stock has risen in price, your option becomes more valuable. Therefore, you can profit by selling your option (cost $500) for the current market price. However, what if the stock price fell to $20 per share? You could let your option expire and lose $500 or sell your option at a reduced cost, limiting your loss.

Puts are the opposite of calls. You anticipate a share price will drop to $35 per share, so you buy a put (sell) option for 100 shares at $40. Like a call, if you speculate correctly, you will profit. However, if the share price rises you will incur a loss.

That is a brief look at put and call options. Professional traders combine options with complex strategies such as straddles and combinations. For more information about these strategies and options in general, read *Getting Started In Options* (John Wiley & Sons, Inc.), by Michael C. Thomsett.

Pork Bellies Anyone?

Soybeans, pork bellies, and frozen orange juice concentrate are probably the most common types of **commodity futures** known to the public, thanks to the movie industry. Futures are contracts for delivery of specified commodities at a later date. Based on the commodity futures' offering price and delivery date found in the newspaper, an investor speculates whether the offering price will be higher or lower on that date. If an investor speculates that pork bellies will be lower than the current offering price on the delivery date, he/she will buy the contract to sell the commodity at the current price. If they are right, the offering price on the delivery date will be lower, thereby creating a profit. Futures trading is a very volatile market and because it is global, prices are extremely sensitive to world events. Futures trading is for experienced traders with high risk tolerance and a willingness to devote vast amounts of time.

If you would like to know more about commodity futures or pork bellies, read *Winning With the Futures Market* (Probus Publishing Co.), by George Angell.

CHAPTER 6

STOCKS & MUTUAL FUNDS
PART II

THE NEXT STEP:
ANNUAL REPORTS & PROSPECTUSES

One of the most intimidating parts of choosing any investment is reviewing the financial statements, such as the prospectus and annual report. This chapter will explain what can be found in the different financial reports and why they are important. We will also cover basic financial analysis tools. They involve ratios to calculate and questions to ask before investing. These tools, although technical at times, can help you analyze a company. This chapter is more difficult to digest than the others. Do not feel discouraged if you don't get a clear picture on your first try. Read to understand the basic concepts and refer back to this chapter as you start looking at potential investments.

What You Will Find In An Annual Report

Both public companies (companies that issue publicly traded stocks) and mutual funds prepare annual reports. They provide useful information, as long as you know where to look.

Company Annual Reports

Public companies' annual reports commonly begin with a well-written letter from the president to the shareholders. This is where last year's gains are loudly proclaimed, or last year's losses are de-emphasized, explained, or excused. Regardless of past results, the future always looks rosy, full of tremendous plans and the anticipation of high returns. If you are lucky, your annual report will include a picture of the president himself, dressed appropriately in a dark suit and white shirt. The president's letter will generally be followed by graphs summarizing high level information in easy to understand blocks and pies. In some of the more flashy annual reports, the charts and graphs will be in bright bold colors, looking more like a picture book than a financial document.

This is as far as most of us read, because after the beautiful graphs, the type gets smaller, and eventually the pages fill with a sea of numbers. You will usually find brief summaries discussing past and future trends for each product line or service offered. Following this is the reason for an annual report: the financial statements. The thought of a financial statement probably turns you off, but it is important to familiarize yourself with financial summaries. We will be explaining the Balance Sheet, Income Statement, Statement of Cash Flows, Statement of Stockholder's Equity, per-share data and ratios.

Mutual Fund Annual Reports

A mutual fund annual report may also begin with a letter from the president of the mutual fund company. Following the letter is the fund's individual investment holdings and the dollar amount associated with each investment. It is important that you are satisfied with the majority of the investments in the fund's portfolio. For instance, if the mutual fund is heavily into pig investments, and you think next year the world will put a ban on eating bacon, then that could be a sign of a poor investment that may go "pork belly-up." Also contained is a **Statement of Operations** and a **Statement of Changes in Net Assets.** These statements list information such as expenses, net gain or loss on investments, and distributions to shareholders. From these statements, you can get information regarding past returns, trends, and management fees.

What's a Prospectus?

A prospectus is a document which explains the nature of business, risk factors, and various other financial information for a security. An investment, such as a mutual fund or an initial public stock offering (IPO), is required to supply each investor with a prospectus. For established stocks, an annual report is prepared instead of a prospectus. It is important to read a prospectus before you make an investment. In the end, the only person looking out for your best interests is you, so spend the time to fully research your choice. In a mutual fund prospectus, you will find information on total fund operating expenses, investment objectives, fund policies, how to buy shares, and most importantly *risk factors*. In an IPO prospectus, you can find similar information — a brief history about the company, number of shares offered, summary of financials and operating data, dividend policy, future strategies and again, most importantly, *risk factors*. You need to at least thumb through a prospectus to get a general idea of the security. Although it is not the only criteria for a good investment, it will help in your decision making. In other words, doing research is like making sure the pool is full of water before you dive in.

Why Should I Read Financial Statements?

Before this book starts to resemble an Accounting 101 book, let's take time out to explain why reading the financial statements is important. In what type of company do you want to invest? An organization with a strong potential for continuing growth and increased profitability? Correct, but how does one recognize this type of firm as opposed to one on the verge of bankruptcy? You could call the president of the company and ask him if he expects profits to increase over the next five years, but what do you think he will say? "Based on our current projection of increased snow storms for the next five winters, we are very confident that snowshoe sales in the Northeast will skyrocket, sending profits through the roof." Do you believe him? Maybe, but wouldn't you like to know what sales were for the past five years to compare against future estimates? Does the company make a profit from snowshoe sales, or do mukluks have the largest profit margin? What happens if the next five winters bring no snow? Is the company in a good financial position to ride through a bare and dry winter? What if everyone else bought this stock because they also heard the president's optimistic statement, forcing the price up and overvaluing the stock? How does one answer all of these questions? Simple, by analyzing the financial statements. Take your money out from underneath the mattress because we are going to show you how to analyze a financial statement.

Financial Statement Analysis

There are no "sure things." To become an expert in financial analysis requires time, patience, and skill. Even for a professional, "doing the numbers" on a company is not a guarantee of investment success. That aside, it is important to show you some financial ratios that will help you learn more about your potential investments.

First, we need to define some accounting terms. A **Balance Sheet** lists the **assets** (what a firm owns), the **liabilities** (what a firm owes to others) and stockholders' equity, also called **shareholders' equity** or **net worth**, (the difference between what a firm owns and owes). Typical assets might be cash, accounts receivable, inventories, and buildings. Typical liabilities might be accounts payable, salaries payable, income taxes payable, and long-term/short-term debt. Stockholders' equity will list the number of outstanding shares (this means the number of stock **shares** held by the public), the par value per share for common and preferred stock, and **retained earnings**.

The **Income Statement** (also called the **Statement of Earnings**) generally lists total sales, cost of sales, gross margin (the difference between the two), general and administrative expenses, taxes, and net income/loss.

Enough with the Accounting 101 lesson, let's begin the analyzing. The following financial ratios need to be taken together collectively to form an overall picture of the company. Many of these ratios are already calculated for a particular company in *Value Line* and *Standard & Poor's Stock Reports*. An example is provided at the end of the chapter where we perform the next eight steps.

1) INCOME STATEMENT - Percentage Trend Analysis. Divide the dollar amount of each item on the income statement by net sales (total sales minus returns and discounts) to calculate a percentage. Compare these percentages to prior years' percentages to determine significant changes. For example, with technically sophisticated companies, it would be important to track research and development expenses. Is the money spent on research and development increasing over time or is the company cutting back? What if a company is in a highly competitive industry that requires innovative new products each year? If money spent on research and development is decreasing, future profits may not be as good as present day profits. Remember, you want to buy stock in a company poised for growth and continued profitability.

If you are a disbeliever, try looking at the dollar amounts as stated each year. You would probably see sales increasing each year and think it is a growing company. You would probably also see the cost of sales increasing each year. This is nothing to worry about because as sales increase, costs increase. However, what you won't see is the cost of sales is increasing at a higher rate than actual sales. Even if sales have been increasing, it is costing the company more money per sale than in past years. Everyone knows what happens when costs grow faster than sales. . . lower profits!

These percentages can also be compared to industry data. One source of industry information is *Robert Morris & Associates Annual Statement Studies*. All financial data is listed by percentage and is grouped by industry type and company size. For example, if you are analyzing a company that makes electronic parts, you would determine from the *Robert Morris & Associates Annual Statement Studies* index that the company falls under SIC #3671 - Manufacturers - Electronic Components & Accessories. Turn to that section and you will find financial information in percentages sorted by asset size and sales level. Try to match the company to the appropriate asset size or sales level and compare.

2) BALANCE SHEET - Percentage Trend Analysis. Divide the dollar amount of each item on the balance sheet by total assets and develop a percentage. Sound familiar? Compare percentages to prior years and try to identify trends. These percentages can also be compared to industry norms in the *Robert Morris & Associates Annual Statement Studies*.

3) LIQUIDITY. There are two ratios which measure the liquidity of a company (ability to meet current obligations).

The Current Ratio = Current Assets ÷ Current Liabilities

Profits may appear larger if this ratio is too low, but the trade-off is that short term liquidity risk increases.

The Quick Ratio = (Cash + Cash Equivalents + Short Term Inventory + Receivables) ÷ Current Liabilities

Both ratios are calculated from the balance sheet and measure the company's ability to meet its current obligations. These ratios should be compared against similar companies.

4) SOLVENCY. The following ratios measure the solvency of a company (ability to meet long-term obligations).

Debt to Equity Ratio = Total Liabilities ÷ Total Stockholders' Equity

If this ratio is high compared to similar companies, it could be caused by excessive debt, which in turn could create excessive financial risk.

Book Value per Share = Total Stockholders' Equity ÷ Number of Common Shares Outstanding

Both ratios are also calculated from the balance sheet and measure the long run solvency of the company.

5) PROFITABILITY. Here are four ratios which measure the profitability of a company (excess income over costs).

Profit Margin = Net Income ÷ Net Sales

If you have performed step #1, this calculation is already done. Be sure to analyze this percentage over time and try to understand differences that you see. If profit margins have increased steadily for the past five years, there is a good chance that they will continue to increase, which increases the stock's price per share.

Earnings Per Share = (Net Income less Preferred Stock Dividends) ÷ Average Number of Common Shares Outstanding

Price to Earnings Ratio (P/E Ratio) = Price per Share ÷ Earnings per Share

Payout Ratio = Dividends per Share ÷ Earnings per Share

6) DEBT LEVEL.

Fixed Assets to Net Worth = Total Fixed Assets net of Depreciation ÷ Total Stockholders' Equity

If this ratio is increasing over time, it may be caused by excessive purchases of fixed assets (property, plant and equipment), financed by debt. If expansion happens too fast, and is paid for with debt, profits could be hurt. Having debt on a balance sheet is not necessarily bad. You will notice that some companies have no debt while other companies carry both short-term and long-term debt. For each industry, there is an optimal level. Unfortunately, there is no blanket rule as to what it is. Compare this ratio against similar companies within the industry.

7) GROWTH.

Net Sales to Net Worth = Net Sales ÷ Stockholders' Equity

If this ratio is increasing over time, it indicates that the company might have unrestrained growth. Unrestrained growth is not always a positive sign. Profitability could be negatively affected because of insufficient cash to propel further sales. This means the company might not be able to sustain rapid growth during adverse conditions, such as supply problems, inventory problems, or a recession.

8) RETURN TO OWNERS.

Return on Equity(ROE) = Net Income ÷ Stockholders' Equity

If this ratio is too low, the company is not producing a satisfactory return to its owners. In turn, the value of the company could decline. However, an investor should not rely solely on an ROE ratio because of three factors. First, a company may have a low ROE today because it is currently incurring expenses that will benefit it in the future. Second, the ROE is calculated using book value, per the financial statements, rather than current market values. This can result in a large difference. Finally, companies may be incurring excessive amounts of debt which distorts the ratio.

Limitations to Using Ratios

The following section describes five limitations to remember when using ratios.

1) Inflation can overstate company performance. If inflation is low, historical performance is more accurate. During periods of high inflation, such as in the 1970s, sales and costs increased partly due to inflation. This can mislead the investor who has not taken inflation into consideration.

2) When using ratio analysis, there is a danger of using ratios in isolation. There may be compensating advantages that offset poor ratios. For example, suppose profit margin has decreased over the past year. You may think the company is doing poorly; however by investigating further, you may find that the low profit margin is caused by an increase in research and development expenses.

3) Performing ratio analysis on comparative industry data is difficult for conglomerate companies. For example, Sears' financial statements include its various subsidiaries. Some of its subsidiaries include Allstate Insurance, an insurance company, and Coldwell Banker, a real estate company. All of Sears' subsidiaries are categorized differently than its retail department stores. In order to compare Sears against industry data, the financial information would have to be broken down and compared against other department stores, life insurance

companies, auto and home supply retailers, etc. Often, financial information will not be separated on the statements. Use caution when comparing industry data in these instances.

4) Industry data may be compiled from a poor sample of companies. When comparing a company's ratios and percentages against industry averages, it is possible that the industry averages use data from companies with substandard performances. This means that if the company being analyzed has ratios that match industry average ratios, it is performing at the industry average. Unfortunately, this happens to be a poor performance. To avoid this, try using industry average information from reputable sources such as *Robert Morris & Associates Annual Statement Studies*.

5) Financial statement amounts may not be accurate. Pay special attention to financial statements that have to be **qualified**. Look for an **unqualified** opinion in the independent auditor's report. This means that they approve the financial reporting practices without condition. Most publicly traded companies will have unqualified opinions to be in accordance with the S.E.C. (Securities and Exchange Commission) regulations. If it is a qualified opinion, watch out! Be sure to look closely into the reason it is qualified.

Before we end Limitations to Using Ratios, we want to talk about one more point that people ignore when reading financial statements. Read the footnotes. Footnotes, what are footnotes? Footnotes are the only place where Certified Public Accountants can express themselves. Footnotes and/or disclosures contain facts about a company that the reader cannot derive from the numbers. If the company is involved in a lawsuit, for instance, the footnotes should note this and include the likelihood of a favorable or unfavorable judgment, and a conservative estimate of the dollar amount. Any contractual commitments, accounting changes, or restructuring changes should appear in the footnotes. Footnotes will also reveal any unconsolidated subsidiaries and equity investments that the company is involved in.

Research Beyond Financial Statement Analysis

Financial statement analysis is only half the battle when researching a company. Life is never spelled out for anyone in black and white, and a company's stock is no exception. You must step back and look at trends in the industry as a whole, the company's products, services, and position within that industry. Although a company might look good on paper, its industry may have become more competitive. Where once it was the only company providing a product or service, perhaps now it is one of many. Does the public view the products as part of a current trend or out of date? The following section provides a number of concepts "off the annual report" to consider. However, there is no specific reference publication where you will find the information listed. If you follow Investing's Tip #7, and read any of the financial publications listed, you will find valuable information about particular companies. Keep a sharp lookout for the following areas:

Position of the company in the economy. Is the company vulnerable to swings in the domestic economy? For example, if the company being analyzed produces consumer goods, the investor should be aware of what consumers on a whole are doing. Is consumer spending up or is it sluggish?

Vulnerability to foreign competition. It is important to follow world events and take note of foreign competitors. They potentially affect your investment. For example, trade agreements between the United States and other countries could allow expansion into new territories and increase competition from foreign companies.

Vulnerability to technological change. Several industries experience continuous technological advances. One example is computer software. How many of us have bought the latest software package one day, and after six months realized that we are already two upgrades behind? This industry is affected by technological change. Once a superior product is available, older technology becomes obsolete. Hence, consumers will not buy the old products and eventually company sales will be affected negatively.

Competence of management. Some investors choose a company or mutual fund solely on the management, despite company products, services, or holdings. While this may be extreme, there are gifted individuals who can really make a difference. One example is Lee Iacocca and Chrysler. In the early 1980s, Lee Iacocca took Chrysler from near bankruptcy to large profits. Another example is Stuart Sloan. Stuart Sloan took over Egghead Discount Software paying himself a salary of $1 per year plus stock options. Mr. Sloan resigned from Egghead Discount Software after he had increased profits by 14%. He then went to QFC (Quality Food Centers), raising the grocery chain's profit margins to record levels for the industry.

There are many investors who watch particular executives. Over time, you will begin to hear of, and read about, individuals who have a knack for managing businesses. A good place to begin your research is in *Business Week*'s annual edition of "The Business Week 1000." Read the section titled, "Top Executives to Watch" for up and coming stars.

Status of research and development projects. Is the company in question close to releasing a new product? Although it is difficult to determine the status of a company's research and development projects, keep your eyes on *The Wall Street Journal* and other financial publications. But remember, once an article appears, chances are the market has already reacted to the news. The circulation is very substantial and you are not the only person who knows this information.

Market share of the company. Does the company have a dominant **market share**, or a particular niche within the industry? Do they have the ability to maintain that market share? Does a company with a small market share have new products that will enhance their ability to capture a larger percentage of the market?

One way to get a general idea of market share is to call up parents or friends outside of your city. Ask if the product is available at stores in their area. This might sound strange, but before you know it, you have done a rough market survey. We have had great response with this plan because all of our friends get interested in the same company. We have yet to meet anyone who does not show interest in a potential new product. Investing can be much more enjoyable when resources are pooled. However, be wary of those friends who you are close to, but whose investment advice you do not trust. There is always one friend or family member who matches that description. Our advice is to let that advice go in one ear and out the other.

Investment Clubs

There are formal **investment clubs** that meet regularly and pool investors' resources. We do not belong to an investment club; however, we trade ideas, reports, articles, and advice among our friends. Formal investment clubs can be a great idea. The best investment clubs are formed by a group of people with competent investing knowledge, who are currently striving toward similar goals. There exists an investment club of elderly ladies who have been together for a number of years, and they average a remarkable rate of return on their investments. That is an example of an excellent investment club. The members are approximately the same age and work towards a similar goal.

In order to receive assistance on investment decisions, Jane's mother joined an investment club. However, her investment club consisted of members with age differences spanning more than 30 years. She ended up following the investment advice of a 35 year-old man who happened to be the loudest talker. She is close to retirement (although she doesn't look a day over 30), has very different investment objectives, and follows different tax regulations. Investments must be customized to fit *your* needs, so it is important to choose your club carefully. We convinced her to leave that group if she ever wanted to retire with a Porsche 911.

If you consider joining an investment club, shop around and find a club with similar investment goals. Also, use this book as your investment handbook, and do not let the loudest talker be your guide. If you would like to start your own club, contact the **National Association of Investment Clubs** for assistance ((313) 543-0612).

Bankruptcy Indicators

There are no definite indicators to warn you of upcoming bankruptcy until a company actually declares, and then it is too late for your investment. However, the following can indicate potential business problems. Companies close to declaring bankruptcy may try to hide the fact by coming up with excuses and rationalizations. Do not believe all of the people, all of the time. Here are some possible bankruptcy warning signs:

1) **Unstable earnings** - If earnings are fluctuating dramatically over time, it may be an indication that the company does not have sufficient control over sales and expenses. Too many months of low earnings could put a financial strain on paying off company liabilities and thereby force the company into bankruptcy.

2) **Poor or inexperienced management** - As discussed before, management makes a difference. A company's continued success is determined by competent management. We say "continued success" because there are people with great business ideas, who can start up a new company, but lack the management skills to continue the business successfully. Research top level executives whenever you can. When you begin to invest, you probably won't recognize any names, but store them in the back of your mind. There might come a day when those names will appear favorably or unfavorably in articles or reports. A company's top level executives will be listed on the back page of the annual report and on the Compact Disclosure computer system at your library.

3) **Top management suddenly resigns or sells significant shares of stock** - This could be another indicator that a company is in trouble. When the people who prob-

ably know best are jumping ship and dumping their shares overboard, watch out! If top management does not have faith in the stock price, why should you? If you retain your shares, be sure to have a good reason.

4) **New competition** - When competition enters a market, it could be a sign that the industry is not fulfilling a consumer desire. It can also mean that the industry has growth potential. Either way, this can be detrimental to the existing company. If their products become obsolete or they are not prepared for competition, sales figures and profitability may suffer.

5) **Retail stores always seem to be overstocked and market share is declining** - Shoppers will love this. First of all, you do not have to read any financial statements. Second, there is a possibility for bargain basement prices at a liquidation sale. If the company you are analyzing sells retail goods, take a look around while you shop. Take notice if consumers seem to be buying products or if the display shelves are full. This could be a potential warning sign.

Everything Above Condensed Into an Example

OK, after that section you might have tossed our book among old copies of *People* magazine. We hope not. No, you don't have to remember all the points mentioned above, but think back over the concepts. What do they all have in common? Pure, simple *common sense*, which everyone possesses. Bottom line: does the investment make sense to you and match the level of risk you desire? Let's walk through an example of how to analyze our favorite public company, Tim's Trattoria, Inc. (this is a fictitious name). Tim's Trattoria restaurant chain, located in over 50 different cities, only serves the finest in spaghetti with meatballs (actually, that is all they serve).

The first two charts contain the financial and ownership information for Tim's Trattoria, Inc. The first step is to gather all available information about a company. Our comments and calculations for this example are written in bold italic. As long as the documents are your own property, not the library's, write your comments and calculations directly on the page. This will make it easier for you to perform analyses. First, we wrote down the 52-week high and low stock price found in *The Wall Street Journal*. Tim's Trattoria (TIMT)'s current price of 7 3/4 tends toward the 52-week high stock price of 8 1/8. We also read that a prominent brokerage firm had upgraded TIMT from a **hold** to a **buy.** This upgrade was released one week ago and spurred buying to 8 1/8. Next, we were happy to see a large percentage of stock shares held by officers and directors. Human nature tells us that if management has a financial vested interest in the company, they will do their best to increase the value of their investment. It also demonstrates their commitment to the company's future. We see sales rising, but net income falling on the Five Year Summary of Sales (located at the bottom of the first chart). We mark this point with a question because we will have to further analyze how costs are behaving for 1992. In the ownership section (at the top of the second chart), we did not notice any drastic changes in shares held by institutions or insiders. Chances are, both of these groups know the most current information, so if they are selling significant amounts of

TIM'S TRATTORIA, INC.

52 Week

Low	_High_
6	8 1/8

Ticker Symbol: TIMT

The brokerage firm of "Buy Low Sell High," upgraded TIMT from a hold to a buy on 5/25. Price went from 7 3/4 to 8 1/8. Closed 5/26 at 7 3/4.

Primary SIC Code: 5812 Eating Places

Description of Business: Operates Tim's Trattoria restaurants across the nation, specializing in spaghetti like Grandma used to make.

Current Outstanding Shares as of 3/31/93:	12,650,000	
Shares Held By Officers & Directors:	8,250,000	*65% (8,250,000 / 12,650,000) held by Officers & Directors.*
Number of Shareholders:	2,000	*Shows management has confidence in the company.*
Number of Employees:	1,448	

Fiscal Year End: Mar-31

Auditor: The Ten Keyers
Auditor's Report: Unqualified
Legal Counsel: Perry Mason

Five Year Summary ($ in 000's)

Date	Sales	Net Income	EPS	
1992	$149,350	$5,500	0.42	*Sales are increasing, however net income is decreasing.*
1991	$143,050	$7,500	0.55	*Is there a problem controlling expenses?*
1990	$99,200	$7,350	0.53	
1989	$70,900	$4,900	0.36	
1988	$59,900	$4,400	0.33	
Growth Rate	25.6%	5.9%	4.9%	

OWNERSHIP:

Type	Date	Owners	Change	in 000's Held	% Own	
Institutions	12/31/92	4	33	932	7.19%	*Low percentage of institutional holders. Helps reduce*
5% owners	3/31/93	1		386	2.98%	*the risk of "dumping" shares which can cause*
Insiders	2/28/93	2		4,087	31.57%	*extreme price fluctuations. Creates a better*
						environment for the small investor.

INSTITUTIONAL OWNERSHIP:

Name	Rank	Latest Qtr Chg in Shs	Shares Held	Date	
Guido's Gun Emporium	1	0	171,000	12/31/92	*Important to note the latest quarter change in*
Italian State Teachers Retirement	2	1,675	130,000	12/31/92	*shares. This gives an idea of how current*
New York State Mafia Retirement	3	(3,750)	113,500	12/31/92	*shareholders feel about the future.*
Godfather's Insurance Co	4	35,075	517,500	12/31/92	
Total		33,000	932,000		

5% OWNERSHIP:

	Location	Shares Held	Date	
Tim	U.S.	3,859,500	12/31/91	*You can run a search on Tim to see*
				ownership history.

INSIDER OWNERSHIP:

	Rank	Latest Trade	Shares Held	Date	
Tim	1	0	3,858,500	5/1/92	*Tells the activity of insiders. If they were all*
Tim's Grandma	2	(5,000)	228,000	3/1/90	*selling large amounts of shares, then*
Total		(5,000)	4,086,500		*WATCH OUT!*

their shares, we do not want to be buying.

Balance Sheet & Income Statement (Example)

The next three charts show the balance sheet and income statement. Notice that for each year, we took balance sheet amounts as a percentage of total assets, and income statement amounts as a percentage of net sales in order to show relative changes in each line item. We then compared key line items of the financial statements against industry averages found in *Robert Morris & Associates Annual Statement Studies.* They were located under SIC code #5812, Eating Places. Look at current assets, intangibles, current liabilities, and long-term debt on the balance sheet. The percentage of total current assets to total assets is much lower for TIMT than industry average. This could cause a potential problem in paying current obligations. Later, we will calculate the current and quick ratio to analyze this further. Notice intangibles are a higher percentage than industry average. An intangible is a nonphysical asset that has value for a business. We know why TIMT has a high proportion of intangibles. Five years ago, the restaurant chain purchased the exclusive rights to "The Super Pasta Maker Machine," which can produce fresh pasta at a rate of 10 lbs. per hour. This exclusive right is valued at $15,000,000 per year. Next, notice that current liabilities are well below industry average. This limits short-term problems in paying obligations. Although there is a low proportion of current liabilities, there is a significant amount of long-term debt.

The income statement for the year ending 3/31/92 is close to the industry average. In fact, net income before taxes is higher than industry average. However, notice the 2% increase in cost of goods sold from the year ending 3/31/91 to 3/31/92. This may not seem like a huge increase, but notice how it affects the bottom line through a reduction in net income.

BALANCE SHEET (ASSETS)

Industry Average	Balance Sheet in $000's	3/31/92	% of total assets	3/31/91	% of total assets	3/31/90	% of total assets
	Assets:						
4%	Cash	$3,000	*3%*	$4,200	*4%*	$4,350	*5%*
4%	Marketable Securities	N/A		N/A		N/A	
6%	Receivables	450	*0%*	750	*1%*	350	*0%*
5%	Inventories	1,300	*1%*	2,250	*2%*	1,050	*1%*
	Raw Materials	N/A		N/A		N/A	
	Work in Progress	N/A		N/A		N/A	
	Finished Goods	N/A		N/A		N/A	
	Notes Receivable	N/A		N/A		N/A	
	Other Current Assets	750	*1%*	1,000	*1%*	800	*1%*
22%	Total Current Assets	$5,500	*5%*	$8,200	*8%*	$6,900	*8%*
	Property, Plant & Equipment	$73,350	*71%*	$66,150	*66%*	$66,500	*77%*
	Accumulated Depreciation	N/A		N/A		13,550	*16%*
63%	Net Property & Equipment	73,350	*71%*	66,150	*66%*	52,950	*62%*
5%	Intangibles	20,600	*20%*	21,350	*21%*	22,150	*26%*
	Deposits & Other Assets	3,750	*4%*	4,750	*5%*	3,950	*5%*
	Total Assets	$103,200	*100%*	$100,450	*100%*	$85,950	*100%*

If you see an impressive jump in one line item, don't overlook offsetting changes in other line items. For example, selling marketable securities and increasing debt to make capital purchases.

BALANCE SHEET (LIABILITIES)

	Balance Sheet in $000's	3/31/92	% of total assets	3/31/91	% of total assets	3/31/90	% of total assets
Industry Average							
	Liabilities:						
	Notes Payable	N/A		N/A		N/A	
	Accounts Payable	6,400	6%	6,050	6%	6,250	7%
	Current Long Term Debt	400	0%	400	0%	450	1%
	Accrued Expenses	5,200	5%	4,150	4%	5,850	7%
	Income Taxes	N/A		N/A		N/A	
30%	Total Current Liabilities	$12,000	12%	$10,600	11%	$12,550	15%
	Deferred Charges / Income	$4,700	5%	$4,200	4%	$4,150	5%
26%	Long Term Debt	42,950	42%	43,150	43%	27,600	32%
	Non Current Capital Leases	N/A		N/A		5,650	7%
	Total Liabilities	$59,650	58%	$57,950	58%	$49,950	58%
	Preferred Stock	N/A		N/A		N/A	
	Common Stock	150	0%	50	0%	50	0%
	Capital Surplus	11,200	11%	11,400	11%	11,350	13%
	Retained Earnings	37,650	36%	32,100	32%	24,600	29%
	Treasury Stock	(5,450)	-5%	(1,050)	-1%	N/A	
39%	Shareholder Equity	$43,550	42%	$42,500	42%	$36,000	42%
	Total Liabilities & Net Worth	$103,200	100%	$100,450	100%	$85,950	100%

Increase in long-term debt corresponds to increase in interest expense. This could lead to short term cash flow problems in the future.

INCOME STATEMENT

Income Statement in $000's	3/31/92	% of net sales	3/31/91	% of net sales	3/31/90	% of net sales	
			Fiscal Year Ending				
Industry Average							
Net Sales	$149,350	100%	$143,050	100%	$99,200	100%	
Cost of Goods	83,050	56%	77,800	54%	52,000	52%	*Increase in cost of goods sold*
44% Gross Profit	66,300	44%	65,250	46%	47,200	48%	*compared to sales may represent management's*
R & D Expenditures	N/A		N/A		N/A		*inability to control costs.*
Selling General & Admin	52,550	35%	50,400	35%	34,350	35%	
6% Income before Depreciation	13,750	9%	14,850	10%	12,850	13%	
Depreciation	N/A		N/A		N/A		
Non-operating Income	(1,800)	-1%	(100)	0%	200	0%	
Interest Expense	3,350	2%	3,150	2%	1,750	2%	
4% Income before Taxes	8,600	6%	11,600	8%	11,300	11%	*Notice the effect a 2% point change*
Provision for Income Taxes	3,100	2%	4,100	3%	3,950	4%	*in cost of goods sold can have on net income before taxes.*
Net Income	$5,500	4%	$7,500	5%	$7,350	7%	
Outstanding Shares in 000's	13,200		13,600		13,800		

Financial Ratios (Example)

In the last part of the example, are the key financial ratios.

Earnings Per Share (.42) - Profitability per share has decreased from the year ending 3/31/91 to 3/31/92. This is due to an increase in cost of goods sold for the year ending 3/31/92.

Price to Earnings Ratio (16.2) - This ratio has been increasing which suggests that investors anticipate higher earnings. TIMT has an average P/E ratio (16.2) compared to the industry (16.1).

Payout Ratio - This ratio cannot be calculated on Tim's Trattoria, Inc. because no dividends are paid on this stock.

Profit Margin (.06) - The profit margin is higher than industry average, but it has been decreasing each year. This is due to an increase in cost of goods sold.

Current Ratio   (.46) - The current ratio has decreased for the year ending 3/31/92. Compared to the industry, it falls between the lower and medium quartile (explained below). This could indicate a possible problem meeting short-term obligations.

Industry information is from *Robert Morris & Associates Annual Statement Studies*. The lower, medium, and upper quartile are different from an average amount. Lower quartile figures represent the lowest 25% ratios, medium quartile figures represent the middle 50% ratios, and upper quartile figures represent the upper 25% ratios.

Quick Ratio (.40) - The quick ratio has also decreased for the year ending 3/31/92, but it falls in the medium quartile for the industry.

KEY FINANCIAL RATIOS

		Average		3/31/92	3/31/91	3/31/90	*Ratios can be found in the following sources:*
			Profitability Ratios:				
			Earnings Per Share (EPS) after tax	0.42	0.55	0.53	*CD ROM*
		16.1	Price to Earnings Ratio	16.20	10.43	8.92	*CD ROM*
			Payout Ratio	No Dividends Paid			
		0.04	Profit Margin (income before taxes)	0.06	0.08	0.11	*Income Statement*

Upper Quartile	*Medium Quartile*	*Lower Quartile*					
			Liquidity Ratios:				
1.1	*0.6*	*0.3*	Current Ratio	0.46	0.77	0.55	*CD ROM*
0.8	*0.4*	*0.2*	Quick Ratio	0.40	0.68	0.46	*CD ROM*
			Coverage Ratios:				
0.9	*1.9*	*4.0*	Debt to Equity	1.37	1.36	1.39	*CD ROM*
			Book Value per Share	3.30	3.13	2.61	*Value Line*
			Financing of fixed assets:				
1.1	*2.0*	*3.4*	Fixed Assets to Net Worth	1.68	1.56	1.85	
			Growth Ratio:				
			Net Sales to Net Worth	3.43	3.37	2.76	
			Stockholder's return:				
			Return on Equity (ROE) after tax	0.13	0.18	0.20	*CD ROM*

Debt to Equity (1.37) - The proportion of debt to equity has remained steady for the past three years. It falls between the medium and upper quartile for the industry. It does not appear that TIMT has excessive debt.

Book Value per Share (3.30) - The book value per share has been steadily increasing. This is a positive sign for the future.

Fixed Assets to Net Worth (1.68) - This ratio falls between the medium and upper quartile for the industry. It does not appear that expansion is happening too fast.

Net Sales to Net Worth (3.43) - This ratio has been increasing gradually each year which indicates good growth potential.

Return on Equity (.13) - This ratio has been decreasing for the past three years. This is not a positive sign for the investor. We know that for the year ending 3/31/92, ROE is low due to increased cost of goods sold. Last night, we heard that tomato prices for the first quarter of 1992 were the highest they had ever been for 10 years, but were expected to fall due to an anticipated boom crop of tomatoes. What do you think would be a large cost for a restaurant specializing in spaghetti? Could it be tomatoes? This would explain the increase in cost of goods sold. If the experts are correct, and tomato prices drop, return on equity, earnings per share, and profit margin could rise for the year ending 3/31/93.

Although we did not include footnotes for Tim's Trattoria, Inc., be sure to read them where available. Tim's Trattoria looks like a good investment if the prices of tomatoes drop. Be sure to look ahead into the future. Besides tomatoes, what is another large cost of operating a restaurant? Labor? Could Tim's Trattoria, Inc. be affected by health care reforms?

If Tim's Trattoria was an actual public company, the information listed on the previous pages could have come from the Compact Disclosure computer system. Annual reports sent out by the company are not the only place to find financial information about a company. *Standard & Poor's*, *Moody's*, and *Value Line Investment Survey* also give financial information. *Value Line Investment Survey* and *Standard & Poor's Stock Reports* also give a synopsis about the company's future.

CHAPTER 7

BONDS

What is the first thing that comes to people's minds when they think of **bonds**? Junk bonds, Michael Milken, and the scandal that went along with them, but there is more. This chapter will describe how the bond market works, and discuss six types of bonds: corporate, U.S. government, state and municipal, mortgage-backed, U.S. savings, and zero coupon. While stocks are equity issues (owning a portion of a company), bonds are debt issues (loaning money to an institution). Just think of a bond as an IOU from a company or some branch of government (federal, state or local). Bonds can be a great addition to your portfolio. They are generally considered less risky than equity issues because if a company declares bankruptcy, bondholders are paid before stockholders. By investing a portion of your portfolio in bonds, you can enhance diversification among different securities.

Bonds come in different sizes to match investors' needs. Short-term bonds mature in less than two years, intermediate-term bonds mature in two to 10 years, and long-term bonds mature in more than 10 years. When you are buying bonds, you are investing for a guaranteed income. This is because bonds pay a fixed amount twice a year. This amount is determined by the stated **coupon rate** or interest rate. The interest paid out never changes through the life of the bond. For example, a $1,000 bond with a coupon rate of 10% pays $50 every six months ($100 per year). Issuers of the bond are required to pay back the full purchase price at a particular date called the **maturity date**. Let's use the same example above, but assume you bought the bond in the open market for $1,100. This would mean that you bought the bond at a **premium**. However, if current market conditions allow you to buy the bond at $800, this would be a **discount**. Regardless, you will still receive the same interest payments at $100 per year. At the maturity date, which could be in 30 years, you will receive $1,000 **par value** for the bond. An $800 bond paying $100 per year, produces a **current yield** of 12.5%. The current yield is the rate of interest based on the current price of the bond. You will also hear the term **yield to maturity**. This is different from the current yield because it factors in the difference between the purchase and selling price at the time the bond matures.

Why and How Bond Prices Move

After bonds have been issued, they do not stay at the

same price in the open market. Bond prices are affected by several factors including interest rates. As interest rates go up, bond prices fall. This represents an inverse relationship. As interest rates fall, bond prices rise. You will notice that only bond prices are changing while the amount of interest that a bond pays out each year remains constant. The following table shows how bond prices and current yields change in relation to interest rates. Assume a new bond is issued for $1,000 par value with an interest rate of 10%.

	Interest Rate	Bond Price	Current Yield	Interest Payment
Older Bond		769	13%	100
Older Bond		833	12%	100
Older Bond		909	11%	100
New Issue		**$1,000**	**10%**	**$100**
Older Bond		1,111	9%	100
Older Bond		1,250	8%	100
Older Bond		1,429	7%	100
Older Bond		1,667	6%	100

As interest rates rise, companies issue new bonds at higher interest rates. Let's say this higher interest rate is 11%, producing an interest payment of $110 ($1,000 x 11%). Since the older bond's interest payment stays the same ($100), the impact will be on the older bond's price. Price could fall to $909 so that the current yield would equal 11%. The opposite scenario happens when interest rates fall.

Companies might issue new bonds at a lower interest rate, for example 9%. On a $1,000 par value bond, 9% interest rate equals $90 in interest payments. In order for the older bond to have a current yield of 9%, the price would have to increase to $1,111. Bonds rise and fall in price depending upon the availability of new bonds issued at a higher or lower interest rate. If new bonds pay more interest, older bonds fall in price because they are less desirable. The opposite happens if new bonds pay less interest. Older bonds rise in price because they are in higher demand. Do not let this confuse you. It makes sense that prices fall and rise to meet demand. From the example below, you would choose the bond paying 10% interest (if the price was the same), rather than the bond paying 8% interest.

	Interest Rate	Interest Payment
Original Issue Bond (par value = $1,000)	8%	$80
New Issue Bond (par value = $1,000)	10%	$100

In order for the 8% interest-paying bond to compete with the 10% bond, the price must fall to where the two bonds have equal current yields.

A bond's interest rate is affected by the length to maturity. For example, a 30-year bond will have a higher interest rate than a two-year bond with similar characteristics. You need to decide if the difference between long-term and short-term interest rates is large enough to justify the added risks. By holding a longer term bond, you may risk incurring a loss due to inflation and interest rate fluctuations.

Rating Bonds

A bond's rating will also affect the bond's interest rate. The rating is as follows: double thumbs up for a highly-rated bond and double thumbs down for a low-rated bond! (Just kidding.) On the next page are the true bond quality ratings as defined by *Standard & Poor's* and *Moody's Investors Service*. Bonds are rated from triple-A, being the best, to D, being in default. A bond with a high rating should offer a lower interest rate than a bond with a low rating. This makes sense when you understand that the rating is based on the issuer's ability to repay the interest and principal (original investment) on the debt (bond). Bond ratings should be a factor in your purchasing decision. A bond issue with a lower, riskier rating needs to offer higher interest rates. How else would they lure investors from safer investments? We have separated the bond ratings by investment grade and speculative grade. It is difficult to assign a rating to speculative grades. You should concentrate on buying investment grade bonds if you are risk averse.

Always remember that bond ratings are not set in stone. *Standard & Poor's* and *Moody's* update their ratings periodically. An issuer can initially have a single A rating and later be downgraded to a triple B rating.

For more information on bonds, read *How the Bond Market Works*, by the New York Institute of Finance.

BOND RATINGS

Standard & Poor's	Moody's	
		INVESTMENT GRADE
AAA	Aaa	Highest rating with extremely strong capacity to pay interest and principal.
AA	Aa	Very close to the highest rating with a very strong capacity to pay interest and principal.
A	A	Strong capacity to pay interest and principal, but are more susceptible to changing economic climates. Referred to as upper medium grade.
BBB	Baa	Adequate capacity to pay interest and principal for the present, however they may be unreliable over time. Referred to as a medium grade.
		SPECULATIVE GRADE
BB	Ba	Speculative assurance of interest payments and principal repayment.
B	B	Small assurance of interest payments and principal repayment. Generally involve a higher degree of risk.
CCC	Caa	Poor standing with danger of default.
CC	Ca	Highly speculative, often in default.
C	C	Lowest rating class of bonds with extremely poor assurance of repayment.
D		In default and behind on payments of interest and principal.
+,-	1,2,3	Relative standings within each category with 1 or + representing the higher end and 3 or - representing the lower end.

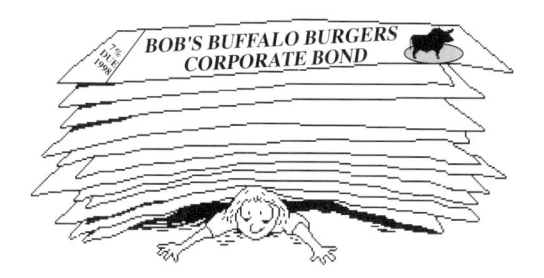

CORPORATE BONDS

This section will define corporate bonds and show you how to do your own research. Corporations issue bonds to raise capital for a variety of reasons. **Corporate bonds** are usually sold in $1,000 units; however, there are **baby bonds** that sell for under $500. Just to be confusing, bonds selling for $1,000 are quoted in $100 units. This is easy to get around. Just add a zero to the end of the price. For example, a bond quoted in the newspaper at $105 is selling for $1,050. Also quoted in the newspaper are the stated interest rate, maturity date, current yield, trading volume, closing price, and percentage change. Take a look at the following example:

Issuer	Interest Rate	Maturity Date	Current Yield	Volume	Closing Price	Net Change
Kmart	8 3/8	17	7.9	10	105 5/8	+1/8

The issuing corporation is Kmart. The annual interest payment you will receive on a $1,000 par value bond is $83.75 ($1,000 x 8.375%). The bond's maturity date is the year 2017. The current yield, which is the interest rate earned on the current price of the bond, is 7.9% ($83.75 annual interest payments ÷ $1,056.25 current price of bond). Volume of bonds traded for the day was 10,000. The closing price is $1,056.25, up $1.25 from the day before. If you bought this bond today, you would be buying at a premium. From our bond price example before, it makes sense that the bond would sell at a premium because the current yield has fallen from 8.375% to 7.9%.

Let's take another look at the bond's maturity date. You will notice that we called 2017 the bond's maturity date. However, the bond will not automatically mature on that date because many bond issuers put call provisions (the call date) in their bonds. The **call date** entitles the issuer to buy out their existing debt before the maturity date, in order to refinance at a lower interest rate. When interest rates fall, bond issuers may exercise their call option. The same principal applies to the home mortgage market. When interest rates fall, home owners have the opportunity to refinance their home mortgage loan at a lower rate. This in turn lowers their monthly mortgage payment. Be sure to find out if your bond is callable and factor the call date into your buying decision. If you buy a bond for a long-term investment, you can buy "call protection" which guarantees that the bond will not be called for a specific number of years.

Bonds can also be convertible. No, they are not good for cruising with the rag top down. A **convertible bond** can be traded in for shares of stock in the company that issued the bonds. Bonds that have a conversion feature are usually less sensitive to interest rate fluctuations. An acronym associated with convertible bonds is SIREN or Step-up Income Redeemable Equity Note. SIRENs are intermediate-term, convertible bonds that have two coupon rates. The interest rate begins below market interest rates for a few years, then "steps-up" to a higher rate until maturity. These bonds can also be converted into common stock at a predetermined price. If the common stock does well, your investment profits. If the stock collapses, your investment is safe as long as you did not convert the bond into common stock. What's the catch? The first drawback is the call provision mentioned above. Issuers can call the bond at the time of the step-up, paying a small premium over par. You then have 30 days to convert the bond to common stock. If the stock does not rise, you have given up several years of earning market-rate interest. In this instance, you would have been better off with a regular bond. Second, if the common stock does perform well, you will make a profit, but not as much as if you had bought common shares to start.

Researching Corporate Bonds

So how do you research bonds on your own? The two best sources are *Moody's* and *Standard & Poor's*, both of which have similar information. If we looked at the Kmart Corporation section in *Moody's*, we would see a brief history of the business, list of subsidiaries, officers and directors, consolidated income statement and balance sheet. Also included is a list of Kmart's long-term debt, where we would find the bond that relates to the previous example, under #4 Kmart Corp., debenture 8 3/8s, due 2017. **Debenture bonds** are backed by a company's financial well being, while a **collateralized bond** is backed by specific assets such as equipment or property. Debenture bonds can offer higher rates of return compared to collateralized bonds of similar maturities because the risk of default is often higher.

When buying a bond, you can either buy a new issue or an older issue on the open market. From the discussion above, older issues will either be bought at a premium or a discount. If you buy a new issue, the issuing company pays the broker fees. Buying an older issue requires paying a commission. Most bonds are not traded on the New York and American Stock Exchanges, but are traded in the over-the-counter market.

GOVERNMENT TREASURY BONDS, BILLS & NOTES (TREASURIES)

This section will describe **Treasuries** and tell you how to buy them. The government issues Treasury bills, notes, and bonds to finance the deficit and other spending. It is easy to distinguish between the three types of Treasuries; the difference is the length to maturity.

Treasury Bills, or T-bills as they are more commonly known, come in 13-week (three months), 26-week (six months) and 52-week (one year) maturities. T-bills require a minimum investment of $10,000; however, instead of paying interest, they are sold below face value at a discount. For example, if a six month T-bill is quoted at 2.98, the security would sell for $10,000 minus a 2.98% discount ($298). You would pay $9,702 ($10,000 less $298) for the T-bill. At the end of six months, you would receive the original investment ($9,702) plus interest earned ($298), which equals the original discount. This transaction would give you a 3.07% return ($298 divided by $9,702).

Treasury Notes have maturity terms from two to 10 years. They require a $5,000 minimum investment for terms less than five years and $1,000 for terms greater than five years. Notes pay interest semiannually and guarantee a fixed rate of return. For example, a $1,000 five year note (interest rate of 4%) yields $20 every six months plus the $1,000 at the end of five years.

Treasury Bonds have maturities between 11 and 30 years. Similar to Treasury notes, they pay interest semi-annually, guarantee a fixed rate of return, and require a $1,000 investment. We discussed earlier that corporate bonds can be called before their maturity date. Most Treasury securities are not callable until the last few years. This is an advantage to the investor.

	Maturity Lengths	Minimum Investment
Treasury Bills	3 Months	$10,000
	6 Months	$10,000
	1 Year	$10,000
Treasury Notes	2 to 5 Years	$5,000
	5 to 10 Years	$1,000
Treasury Bonds	11 to 30 Years	$1,000

How to Buy Treasuries

Treasuries can be purchased three ways. First, there is always a broker (discount or full service) who will be more than happy to sell you Treasuries (generally for a fee of $30 to $50). Second, you can buy Treasuries through some banks (also for a fee). Third, Treasuries can be bought directly through the mail or from one of the twelve branches of the Federal Reserve Bank (Atlanta, Boston, Chicago, Cleveland, Dallas, Kansas City, Minneapolis, New York, Philadelphia, San Francisco, St. Louis and Richmond).

Before you buy a Treasury, you need to know when they are auctioned. Three month and six month Treasury bills are auctioned every Monday. When Monday is a holiday, they are auctioned on Tuesday. Auctions determine the interest rate that investors will realize, not the price. Twelve month Treasury bills, two year notes, and five year notes are auctioned once a month. Notes and bonds with three year or more than five year maturities are auctioned quarterly except for 30 year bonds which are auctioned semiannually.

An interested investor needs to open a Treasury Direct Account. The interest earned from Treasury bills, bonds, and notes is automatically deposited into this account. To open an account, write or call the New York Federal Reserve Bank, 33 Liberty Street, New York, N.Y. 10045, (212)-720-6619. Also request instructions on submitting bids by mail. In the submittal, you will need to include a certified check for the full value of the bill, note or bond (you will be refunded later), and indicate whether your bid is non-competitive or competitive. A non-competitive bid accepts the average auction interest rate, while a competitive bid limits the interest rate acceptable. The average auction interest rate is set by competitive bidders. These consist of major financial institutions, mutual funds, pension funds, and insurance companies. Individual investors usually enter non-competitive bids and accept the average auction interest rate.

Treasury securities are the safest form of investment and are considered virtually risk-free because the federal government guarantees payment. They can easily be sold in the **secondary market** and the interest earned is exempt from state and local taxes, but not federal taxes. Because of this insurance, Treasury bonds offer lower yields than corporate bonds. However, if you live in an area with high state and local taxes, be sure to compare Treasury securities' tax advantaged returns to fully taxable alternatives.

STATE AND MUNICIPAL BONDS

As with the federal government, states and cities need to raise money. What it boils down to is that everybody needs money. Anyone could issue an IOU (bond) if they found people to invest. States and cities need money for projects such as schools, roads, and bridges.

Municipal bonds pay interest semiannually and principal at maturity. They usually require an investment between $5,000 and $10,000 and are traded on the over-the-counter market. They can be purchased through major brokerage firms and some banks. Do not skip over this section if the investment requirements look larger than your wallet; there is another option for the amateur investor. Investors with less money can purchase municipal bonds through a municipal bond fund (a type of mutual fund) or a unit investment trust.

You know the definition of a mutual fund, but let's explain a **unit investment trust**. A common unit investment trust consists of a portfolio of municipal bond investments that stay constant until the trust matures. This is different from a municipal bond mutual fund that can continually change its portfolio of municipal bond issues. Unit investment trusts limit the number of shares sold. As soon as all shares have been sold, the unit trust closes to new investors. In simple terms, the investor is locked into a fixed interest rate for the life of the unit trust. When interest rates are low, investors are happy. Unfortunately, when interest rates are rising, investors are disappointed that they are locked into a lower rate. There is typically a minimum investment of $1,000.

The greatest advantage to municipal bonds is that the interest earned is exempt from federal taxes. The interest will also be exempt from your local and state taxes, provided you buy the municipal bond from your state. This enables municipalities to offer lower tax-exempt interest rates to compete against corporate taxable interest rates. Following, is a table comparing the rate of return for taxable and tax-exempt investments. The left column is the tax-exempt percentage return. The three columns to the right represent the taxable return required to match the tax-exempt return. For example, if you are in the 28% federal tax bracket and invest in a municipal bond earning 5%, it would take a taxable investment earning 6.94% to match your municipal bond. To convert tax-exempt yields to taxable yields, use the following equation. Taxable yields (%) = tax-exempt yields (%) divided by [100% - your federal income tax bracket (%)].

Tax Brackets:	15%	28%	31%	36%
Tax-Exempt Yield		Taxable Yields (1)		
5%	5.88%	6.94%	7.25%	7.81%
7%	8.24%	9.72%	10.14%	10.94%
9%	10.59%	12.50%	13.04%	14.06%
11%	12.94%	15.28%	15.94%	17.19%
13%	15.29%	18.06%	18.84%	20.31%
15%	17.65%	20.83%	21.74%	23.44%

(1) Comparable taxable yields will be higher if you live in an area with local and state taxes.

Municipal bonds may be tax-free, but they are not risk-free. Not all municipal bonds are insured or have a federal government guarantee. **General obligation bonds** are backed by the issuer's general taxing power, while **revenue bonds** use the revenue generated by the project (housing, hospitals, etc.) to repay interest and principal. Revenue bonds often pay higher interest because they have a higher degree of risk. There have been situations where municipal bonds have defaulted. One highly publicized example was the Washington Public Power Supply System, better known as WPPSS (Whoops). This municipal bond defaulted when a nuclear power project went bankrupt. There are plenty of cities and states in enough financial trouble to treat this situation carefully. Be sure to purchase municipal bonds that have a high rating and are also insured or backed by the federal government. Remember, municipal bonds are not risk-free.

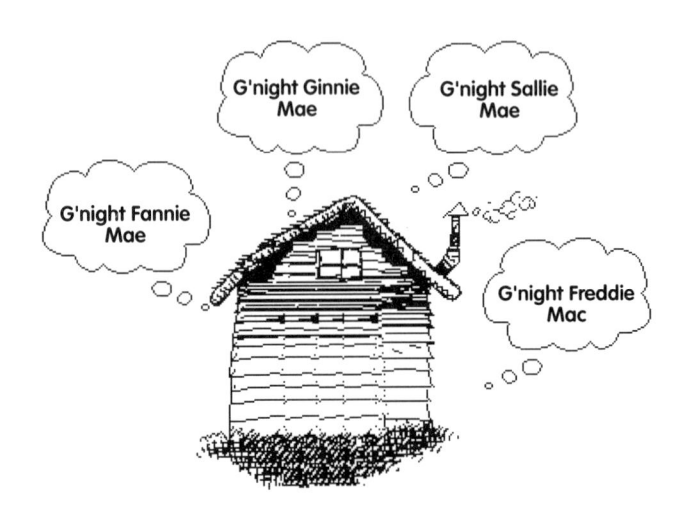

MORTGAGE-BACKED SECURITIES

The title of this section may not look familiar, but you have probably heard the more common names. "Ginnie Mae, Fannie Mae, and Freddie Mac." No, these are not the names of two sweet grandmothers and a grandfather, but the titles of three agencies that offer mortgage-backed securities. If you have ever purchased a home, you probably heard the loan officer speak of Ginnie Maes and Fannie Maes.

Government National Mortgage Association (GNMA or "Ginnie Mae") bonds consist of pools of home mortgages. Investors receive monthly payments of principal and interest as homeowners pay off mortgage principal and interest each month. They require a minimum investment of $25,000 and have 30-year maturity terms; however, they usually have an average life of 12 years. The simple reason is that people often refinance or sell their previous homes, which closes the GNMA early. When mortgages are prepaid, the investor receives part of the original investment. However, investors never know when the principal investment will be repaid. During periods of low interest rates when homeowners are refinancing prepayments usually increase. GNMA bonds are not exempt from any income tax, but are federally guaranteed. Except for fluctuating monthly payments and varying maturity lengths, they are a safe risk-to-return investment. You can purchase GNMA bonds through brokers and many banks. If the $25,000 minimum investment sounds too high, you can always consider a mutual fund that invests in GNMA bonds.

Federal National Mortgage Association (FNMA or "Fannie Mae") bonds resemble GNMA bonds. The only difference is that they require an investment of $10,000. They are backed by federally sponsored mortgages, but are not federally guaranteed. They are considered a moral obligation of the U.S., but not full faith credit.

Federal Home Loan Mortgage Corporation (FHLMC or "Freddie Mac") bonds are pools of single family residential mortgages not guaranteed by FHA (Federal Housing Administration) or VA (Veteran's Administration) in the form of pass-through securities. They are not federally guaranteed as GNMA bonds, but are considered safe investments.

Another government agency that offers **government backed securities** is the Student Loan Management

Agency (SLMA or "Sallie Mae"). SLMA bonds are similar to GNMA and FNMA bonds, but are backed by pools of federally guaranteed student loans. The bonds themselves are also federally guaranteed.

U.S. SAVINGS BONDS

Yes, there is another U.S. government security, **U.S. Savings Bonds**. Series EE Savings Bonds can be used to save small amounts of money in a federally guaranteed investment. These bonds are sold in the following face value amounts: $50, $75, $100, $200, $500, $1,000, $5,000 and $10,000. The bond's purchase price is 50% of the face value. For example, a $100 bond will cost you $50 to purchase. At the end of ten years (EE Savings Bonds' length to maturity), the bond will be worth $100. The investor receives $50 plus the earned interest.

These bonds are designed so that the investor holds the bond for at least five years before selling. This is encouraged because the highest interest rate earned begins after five years. The government also guarantees that this rate will not drop below a predetermined percentage. The bond is not redeemable at all during the first six months. Older Series EE Savings Bonds can be exchanged for Series HH Savings Bonds. Series HH Savings Bonds are bought at par value and earn interest payable twice a year. They have a minimum face value of $500 to $10,000 and mature in 10 years.

You can buy Series EE Savings Bonds at a brokerage firm or some banks. They are exempt from state taxes and deferred from federal taxes until you cash in the bonds. You can also use U.S. Savings Bonds to fund a child's education. Purchase a bond in a child's name to reduce taxes paid. An advantage of the Series EE U.S. Savings Bond is that the interest may be excluded from taxes if the total principal and interest from the maturing bond are used for college tuition. This exclusion may not apply to everyone, so consult a tax advisor or accountant for details.

ZERO COUPON SECURITIES

Zero coupon securities are one way of meeting long-term financial goals. They provide stability through knowing exactly how much they will be worth when they come due. They come in a variety of maturity dates and are exactly what they sound like: securities that pay zero interest until maturity. The interest earned is automatically reinvested so the investor earns interest on both interest and principal. They are sold well below the $1,000 par value and increase in value to $1,000 at maturity. There is no guesswork. You know that at maturity, you will have $1,000 in the bank (less taxes). For example, approximately $53 invested today in a 10%, 30-year zero coupon bond will be equal to $1,000 at maturity. If you have a specific long-term need, such as funding for a future college education, you can buy a 20-year zero coupon security that will mature when your child enters college. You know their value will be $1,000 each, so the planning is easy.

There are different types of zero coupon securities, such as Corporate Zero Coupon Bonds and Municipal Zero Coupon Bonds. Corporate zero coupon bonds are not recommended to individual investors because of higher risk. If the bond does default, your loss is higher because no interest has been received. Be sure to research each type before purchasing.

Zero coupon securities pay interest and principal in one lump sum at maturity, but the government taxes these securities annually as if you were receiving interest payments each year. If you are thinking of zero coupon securities for a child's education, you may want to set up the account in your child's name. This is a great way to save for a child's education on a tax reduced basis.

RETIREMENT INVESTMENTS

As mentioned before, your first investment should be for retirement. That condo in Florida will not come cheap. A common statement heard from both young and not-so-young people is: "It's too early to start thinking about my retirement." Obviously, they haven't heard about the power of compounding. If you start investing $166.67 per month ($2,000 per year) at 10% interest compounded monthly, after forty years it will be worth approximately $1,063,000. Where will those who cannot possibly think about retirement now be in forty years? They will be scrambling to save enough money to pay taxes on their home, while the believer in compounding will be on a beach drinking Mai-Tais out of pineapples.

The following chapter will show you the benefits of **tax-deferred investments** and will describe several types to consider. The greatest advantage of investing for the future is that the government gives an incentive: deferred taxes. In other words, you will receive the benefit of paying taxes at a much later date and hopefully at a lower tax rate. If there is one common thread among investors, it is the aversion to giving a large portion of their hard-earned money to the government. In 1993, there were five different tax brackets: 15%, 28%, 31%, 36%, and 39.6%. To determine your tax bracket, find your income level in the chart below. Over time the exact percentages and amounts may change, but taxes will always exist.

Joint Return		Single Return		Tax Bracket
$0	- $36,900	$0	- $22,100	15.0%
$36,901	- $89,150	$22,101	- $53,500	28.0%
$89,151	- $140,000	$53,501	- $115,000	31.0%
$140,001	- $250,000	$115,001	- $250,000	36.0%
	> $250,000		> $250,000	39.6%

Individuals who claim large tax preference items and deductions (generally higher than $45,000) to their reported income may be affected by the Alternative Minimum Tax (AMT). Please consult a tax advisor or accountant for additional details.

Tax-deferred investments can fall in many categories including IRAs, 401(k)s, 403(b)s, SEP plans, Keough plans, annuities, mutual funds, Treasury securities, and municipal bonds. In this chapter we will talk about the IRA, 401(k), 403(b), SEP plan, Keough plan, and annuities. To understand tax-deferred investments, you must understand the difference between a tax-exempt yield and a taxable yield. Below is the same table comparing tax-exempt and taxable yields as found in the Municipal Bond section. For example, if you are in the 28% tax bracket and invest in an IRA earning 9%, it would take a taxable investment earning 12.5% to match the interest earned on your IRA.

Tax Brackets:	15%	28%	31%	36%
Tax-Exempt Yield		Taxable Yields (1)		
5%	5.88%	6.94%	7.25%	7.81%
7%	8.24%	9.72%	10.14%	10.94%
9%	10.59%	12.50%	13.04%	14.06%
11%	12.94%	15.28%	15.94%	17.19%
13%	15.29%	18.06%	18.84%	20.31%
15%	17.65%	20.83%	21.74%	23.44%

(1) Comparable taxable yields will be higher if you live in an area with local and state taxes.

Yes, taxes make this much difference. In order to match earnings on a 7% tax-exempt investment, you would need to find a taxable investment earning 9.72% (based on a 28% tax bracket). On one hand, do not be fooled by the lower yields of tax-exempt investments, but on the other hand, do not be fooled by individuals who claim their tax-exempt rates are equal to outrageously high taxable yields. Calculate the difference for yourself.

Individual Retirement Account

The first investment we will describe is the Individual Retirement Account, better known as the **IRA**. The IRA is an investment that can be started at a bank, brokerage firm, or mutual fund company. You can contribute up to $2,000 ($2,250 if your spouse does not work) of earned income per year, completely tax-deferred. Your investment earns interest or dividends that are also tax-deferred and reinvested into the IRA.

One advantage of an IRA is that you can start taking your money out of it after retirement (or age 59 1/2) when you are in a lower tax bracket because you are not working. Another advantage of an IRA is that the government dictates how much you can invest, but the investor can decide *where to* invest. This allows you to choose between different conservative investments. You could, for example, choose a conservative mutual fund. Some mutual funds have no minimum to open an IRA account. Other funds, offer low minimum IRA accounts, which require between $100 and $500 to open. Do not invest your IRA in a tax-free investment, such as a U.S. Savings Bond. Why? Because it is redundant. Take taxable investments and turn them into tax-deferred investments using your IRA.

The main disadvantage of an IRA is that there is a 10% penalty if you want access to your IRA before you reach age 59 1/2, become disabled, or die. Another limitation to an IRA is that you must begin taking general distributions from your account no later than April 1 following the year you reach age 70 1/2. This makes an IRA a long-term investment, because you do not want to incur penalties. However, there are certain exceptions to the 10% tax if distributions are part of a scheduled series of substantially equal periodic payments. If you are considering periodic payments, please consult with a tax advisor for more details.

In order to take advantage of a tax deductible IRA, you must include that amount on your yearly tax returns (form 1040 under line 24). If you are covered under an employer's pension plan and your adjusted gross income exceeds $25,000 for singles or $40,000 for couples, you may not claim the $2,000 as tax deductible. However, you can still start a non-deductible IRA and have the interest grow tax-deferred.

401(k) / 403(b) / SEP / Keough Plan

The next tax-deferred investment can be found at work, which tends to surprise people. We all think of work as a place to get coffee and office supplies, and pay large taxes. We need to start thinking of work as the best place for saving taxes. Check to see if your company has a 401(k), 403(b), SEP or Keough plan. Before Uncle Sam takes his share, you can contribute pre-tax income to the appropriate plan. The original investment and interest grow tax-deferred. This way, you save twice. All of these plans follow the same concept as the IRA. Invest as much as you can tax-deferred while you are in a higher tax bracket. When retirement comes, you can withdraw the money at a lower tax bracket. This means paying less taxes over a lifetime.

If you work for a larger corporation, you are more likely to see a **401(k)** plan. 401(k) plans differ from company to company, so be sure to get the details of your company's plan. Some companies match your investment dollar for dollar in a 401(k). Other companies match dollar contributions with shares of stock. Both these options are a great way to invest twice as much as you could otherwise. If your company matches dollar for dollar, you are earning a 100% return. Take advantage of it because this is a great return. "Mai Tais. . . we're coming a little earlier."

These plans normally allow the investor to contribute a percentage of gross salary, usually up to 15% of each paycheck. The maximum yearly dollar limit for 1993 was $8,994. The 401(k) plans have definite advantages over IRAs. A majority let you borrow up to 50% of your total investment at a specific interest rate. The interest paid on the loan is then reinvested back into your 401(k). Many let you select different investment objectives. When you quit or leave your present job, you can either roll over your 401(k) into another company plan or into an IRA. You pay no taxes as long as a direct custodian is assigned to handle the account. You can also cash in your 401(k), but you will pay tax on the total and penalties may be incurred.

Many companies are sprucing up their 401(k) plans as people become more concerned about having enough money for retirement. It is estimated that by the end of the decade total 401(k) assets should reach $1 trillion. This demonstrates the growing future of the 401(k) as an investment for retirement. As they become increasingly popular, we could see increases in the amount employers match, and also greater allowable percentages that employees can put away before being taxed. Keep updated on your company's policy.

The **403(b)** is similar to the 401(k), but is offered for public school employees and employees of certain charitable organizations. These 403(b) plans accepted contributions of 20% of salary or $9,500 per year (whichever is less) in 1993.

SEP (Simplified Employee Pension Plan) and

Keough are tax-deferred plans for people who are self-employed or employees of unincorporated businesses. A Keough plan lets you deduct as much as 25% of your income up to $30,000. A SEP plan lets you deduct as much as 15% of your income up to $30,000. Keough plans have more options than SEP plans, but are more complicated to open and may require a lawyer to start.

Tax-Deferred Annuities

Tax-deferred annuities (TDAs) are investments sponsored by insurance companies. Insurance companies will invest your after-tax money on a tax-deferred basis until you take it out. It's to your benefit to wait until age 59 1/2 to avoid a penalty. TDAs can be an additional way to save for retirement after you have maximized your 401(k) (or equivalent) plan and IRA contributions. TDAs can have high sales loads (initial fees to open a TDA account) and expenses that will affect your rate of return. TDAs can be purchased through insurance agents, brokerage firms, and some banks. They typically have minimum investment amounts between $1,000 and $5,000.

There are two kinds of annuities: fixed and variable. Fixed annuities guarantee a fixed rate of interest for one to five years. Remember, if interest rates are rising you do not want to be trapped in a low rate of return. Variable annuities let you choose a portfolio made up of different securities. The rate of return varies with the performance of the portfolio. TDAs set up with established companies have a low risk of default. Insurance companies' performances are rated by *Best's Rating Service*. Three references that list fixed annuities are *Annuity and Life Insurance Shopper* ((908)-521-5110), *Comparative Annuity Reports* (P.O. Box 1268, Fair Oaks, CA

95628) and *Morningstar Variable Annuity/Life Performance Report* ((800)-876-5005).

If we have not yet convinced you to start spending on your retirement, then turn your doubting eyes to the next example. This table shows what you will have at age 65 if you start spending $2,000 per year in an IRA or 401(k)/403(b)/SEP/Keough. Amounts are rounded and are based on spending $166.67 per month ($2,000 per year) for three different annual rates of return. Notice the difference between beginning at age 25 compared to age 35. At a 10% interest rate, it puts an extra $683,000 in your pocket. This does not even include any employer matching contributions.

	Total Investment at age 65 for:		
Beginning Age	5%	10%	15%
25	$255,000	$1,063,000	$5,234,000
35	$139,000	$380,000	$1,168,000
45	$69,000	$128,000	$253,000
55	$26,000	$34,000	$46,000

Hawaiian surf here we come!!!!

CHAPTER 9

PRECIOUS METALS

GOLD. It is a word that has evoked excitement among people since the days of Christopher Columbus. However, all that glitters may not be gold, especially when describing precious metals. Besides gold, precious metals include silver, platinum, and palladium. (For your information, because we did not know either, palladium is a silver-white metallic chemical element used especially as a catalyst and in alloys.) Precious metals are bought primarily to hedge against high inflation and economic uncertainty. While paper money may lose value during times of high inflation or economic uncertainty, it is believed that metals will hold their value. Holding precious metals in your portfolio can be another way to achieve additional diversification.

Generally, people who have little confidence in the stock market or economy perceive precious metals to be the best investment. However, precious metals can be as volatile as the stock market. In the beginning of 1980, international inflation was high, oil prices were rising, and there was a hostage crisis. These factors and others drove the price of gold to a record high of $887.50 per ounce. People were investing heavily into gold because of the uncertain times. When calmer times returned, the price of gold fell and then stabilized. The gold rush was over. This is an example of how volatile gold prices can be. As with most investments, you must remain attentive. Precious metals are by no means risk-free.

Precious metals are available in bullions or in coins for gold and silver. You can also purchase certificates which hold your precious metals in a secure place. They can be purchased with almost any amount of money, with the exception of certificates, which usually have a $1,000 minimum. You can incur other costs such as storage and insurance. Dealers, brokers, and some banks offer precious metals directly, but another way to invest would be in a precious metal mutual fund. Any gains earned are taxed, and if you live in a state with sales tax, your original purchase of the actual commodity may be subject to sales tax.

CHAPTER 10

LIFE INSURANCE

Do you need life insurance? Not if you are single with no dependents. You cannot use the money after you are gone. However, if you do have dependents, you will want to look into a life insurance plan. Life insurance can be general insurance or it can include an investment program. Some people use insurance investment programs to supplement retirement income; however, the interest rate earned is sometimes not competitive with other investments. We know we have repeated this concept several times, but do your research before investing. We have exposed you to many other investment opportunities, so if the interest rate earned on your life insurance is not up to par with other investments of similar risk, switch to term life insurance and invest your money elsewhere.

Term life insurance, as it is called, is the cheapest and simplest way to get insurance. The premiums pay for the life insurance and do not create any cash value or other investment. **Cash value** (also called straight, whole, permanent or ordinary) life insurance combines the protection of regular life insurance with an investment program. There are typically three programs offered: Universal Life, Variable Life, and Universal Variable Life. Universal life separates the cash value investment portion from the protection portion. It invests the cash value in a tax-deferred savings program tied to a money market rate. Variable life has a fixed premium, but the cash value goes into a choice of stock, bond, or money market portfolios. Universal variable life combines the flexibility of universal life with the growth potential of variable life.

These programs can be purchased through insurance companies, brokers, commercial banks, and financial planners, to name a few. Income earned on the investment is tax-deferred. Here is a helpful tip. A number of insurers have been offering versions of popular term and universal life insurance at a discount. Be sure to ask if this discount is available. If the agent says no, call the insurance company's consumer department and double-check. You may be surprised at the answer.

We have been brief on this subject, but if you want to learn more, read *Life Insurance, A Consumer's Handbook* (Indiana University Press), by Joseph M. Belth.

CHAPTER 11

BANKS

Many people are under the impression that all banks are the same and offer the same services they always have. Not anymore. For instance, they have changed their infamous "bankers' hours." Today, banks are generally open on weekdays from 9:00 a.m. to 6:00 p.m.; some are even open on Saturday mornings. They no longer offer only checking accounts, savings accounts, loans, and certificates of deposit. Banks still offer these standard services, but many also have financial centers that offer a variety of securities, including mutual funds, stocks, and bonds. This chapter will describe to you the importance of choosing the right bank and the investing services they can provide.

What is a Bank and Why Do Some Fail?

It is not uncommon to pick up a newspaper and see an article entitled, "How Safe is Your Bank?" Does this mean you should be paranoid that your bank will fail? In order to answer that question we need to give a brief history lesson about financial institutions. People use the term "bank" to refer to all financial institutions; however, there are several distinct types: commercial banks, savings and loans, and credit unions.

Commercial banks were originally designed to lend only to businesses, but in the early 1900s they began offering accounts to the general public. Savings and loans (S&Ls) originated in 1831. They consisted of individual investors pooling their savings in order to borrow money to build houses and buy material possessions. If you have seen the movie "It's a Wonderful Life," you will remember Jimmy Stewart and the Bailey Building and Loan. This was an example of a S&L. Credit unions pool together money and lend to their members at competitive rates. For example, state teachers have a credit union. Credit unions are not profit-making businesses like commercial banks.

Commercial banks and S&Ls followed different regulations, as dictated by the government, for many years. In the early 1970s, the government began to deregulate the S&Ls in order to improve their financial stability and allow them to compete better with banks. The distinction between the S&Ls and commercial banks began to evaporate. In the early 1980s, restrictions were lessened, increasing the risk of loan default to the lenders. By mid-1980s, land values plummeted and oil prices dropped. Borrowers could not repay their loans and hundreds of banks and S&Ls failed. This left a shortage of funds to reimburse consumers who had invested in regular accounts.

These failed institutions had to be merged with other institutions or bailed out by the government at an enormous cost. In short, the "S&L scandal." Now that we have explained the difference in financial institutions, we will use the term "bank" to refer to all financial institutions.

Back to the original question. Should you be paranoid? Most banks are FDIC (Federal Deposit Insurance Corporation) insured for deposits under $100,000. This means deposits up to $100,000 are guaranteed by the government. There is a small percentage of banks and credit unions that are not insured. Be sure your bank is FDIC insured. For additional information, request the free booklet titled, *Your Insured Deposits* from the FDIC, Office of Consumer Affairs, 550 17th St. N.W., Washington, D.C. 20429.

How Banks Operate

The concept of how a bank makes a profit is simple. Banks bring in funds by offering different accounts and investments, such as savings accounts and certificates of deposit. These are considered the liabilities of the bank because at any time depositors can withdraw money from their account and the bank must pay them. The bank then lends deposited funds to other consumers. Loans are considered assets of the bank because of the interest charged. Banks make a profit by offering a lower interest rate to depositors and a higher interest rate to borrowers.

How To Choose A Bank

You will want to choose a bank that offers the best services to fit your needs. This is not necessarily the closest one to your home or office. But wait a minute, you probably already have a bank. It does not matter. If your bank does not offer the best services, then switch. Banks compete intensely with each other to gain investors, so take advantage of your options. Do not be locked into a certain bank just because you opened your first account there and are sentimentally attached.

As mentioned above, do not take chances on a bank that has uninsured deposits. Make sure your bank is FDIC insured for up to $100,000. Also, if the bank in question is publicly owned, they can provide you with an annual report or financial information. Analyze the bank's financial statements exactly as you would a company's.

Many banks will offer several different kinds of checking and savings accounts. Be sure to read all of the literature, including the small print, before choosing an account. A good question to ask is how their interest rates are compounded. You can see from the chart that follows that interest compounded daily is the most advantageous to you. Not all banks offer daily compounded interest.

	$1,000 compounded at 5% interest				
	1 Year	*5 Years*	*10 Years*	*20 Years*	*30 Years*
Daily	$1,051.27	$1,284.00	$1,648.66	$2,718.09	$4,481.22
Monthly	1,051.16	1,283.36	1,647.01	2,712.64	4,467.74
Quarterly	1,050.95	1,282.04	1,643.62	2,701.49	4,440.21
Semiannually	1,050.63	1,280.09	1,638.62	2,685.06	4,399.79
Annually	1,050.00	1,276.28	1,628.90	2,653.30	4,321.94

Look for banks offering no-fee checking accounts, but be sure to know the rules of how fees can be incurred. For example, your account may be charged each time you use a branch or non-branch ATM (automatic teller machine). Special transactions through the ATM, such as a listing of your most recent transactions, may cost $2 per use. Even *not* using your ATM card might incur a fee. An increasing number of banks are also charging insurance fees as high as $2 per month on deposits. Take notice when your bank is being merged with another bank. The same rules and fees may not carry forward under the merger. Also, research interest-bearing checking accounts. Banks can require a minimum balance in order to earn interest. They will cancel the entire month's interest if the balance drops below the minimum. Ask your bank for a list of all fees and rules that apply to your accounts.

Lastly, it is important to choose a bank that offers free coffee and cookies each time you visit.

Banks Investment Services

A majority of large banks offer investments such as mutual funds, stocks, and bonds, in addition to savings and checking accounts. Ask your banker if a certain security, no matter how specialized, can be bought and sold through your bank. You will probably be surprised by the answer.

Banks have been successful in offering services similar to those you might find at a brokerage firm for several reasons. Many people enjoy doing business with a bank, rather than a full service brokerage firm. You can take care of your banking and investing needs in one location. There is a higher comfort level with a bank because it is less intimidating. Banks instill a sense of trust and security. This is true for your federally insured deposits, but in the mind of the consumer it is sometimes falsely transferred to other investments. If your bank is FDIC insured, deposits up to $100,000 are insured. However, if you purchase shares in a mutual fund, you purchase them with the same level of risk as if you bought them from a brokerage firm. FDIC insurance does not cover non-traditional investments. As with a broker, banks will also charge a fee. The fees may be lower than a full service brokerage firm, but they vary from one bank to another. Be sure to ask up front about all fees.

Certificates of Deposit

Certificates of deposit (more commonly called **CDs**) are investments that offer fixed interest rates for a specified time period. CDs are offered through banks and are insured up to $100,000. They can be purchased in several different maturity lengths, varying from three months to 10 years. The interest rate earned is set at the beginning of the CD's life and is guaranteed until maturity. The longer the CD's term, the higher the interest rate offered. You are locked into an interest rate for the entire time period, regardless of interest rate fluctuations. Therefore, it will be a disadvantage during periods of rising interest rates and an advantage when the opposite occurs. Once you invest in a CD, you must hold it until maturity or pay penalties for early withdrawals. Be sure to check the interest rates offered in order to compare them to the other investments you have read about in this book.

CHAPTER 12

REAL ESTATE

We knew a lady who, on a nurse's salary, invested her money wisely and slowly began to accumulate property. By the time she was 50, she owned five pieces of property valued at approximately $800,000. Not too shabby for a little old lady's retirement. Many people believe that the key to financial wealth can be found through real estate. If you do not already own a home, spending on one could be your second largest priority after retirement.

You can use the investment vehicles we have described to accumulate a down payment. For most of us, it is a dream to buy a piece of property that we can call our own. Real estate can come in the form of a house or condominium, but can also be a vacation house, rental property, or piece of raw land.

Choosing Real Estate

There are three keys to real estate that you must know before buying. These are 1) location, 2) location and 3) location. Even if you have heard this cliche too many times, there is no disregarding the truth it holds. Property sells better, rents higher and appreciates in value more quickly when it is located in a nicer neighborhood. When buying your primary residential home, look for neighborhoods that offer easy commutes to businesses, good schools, indoor and outdoor recreational facilities, and zoning laws that favor the community. If you want to see large appreciation in property value, buy the cheapest house in the nicest neighborhood. Unfortunately, that may be the house with leaky ceilings and an outhouse in the backyard. In that case you may not want to live there, no matter how much appreciation can be gained. In the end, buy the house you will enjoy the most because *you* will have to live there, not your real estate agent (unless of course you really hit it off)!

Real Estate for Sale

Property is either sold through a real estate agency or by the owners. Property listed with a real estate agency will tend to be more expensive because real estate agents take a percentage of the selling price. If a property is listed with an agency, you must go through a real estate agent. It does not have to be an agent with the company that has listed the property. Any real estate agent will do, but you cannot go around the agent and approach the owner with an offer. However, if a property is for sale by owner, then offer away. Finding property today is made much easier with computer technology. Real estate agencies have access to a majority of the property for sale in your area. They can type your requirements into the computer; i.e. three bedrooms, fireplace, deck, and a certain neighborhood. The computer will generate a list of all the properties that match your description. This way you do not have to waste time looking at property with two bedrooms and no deck. It is the same concept as finding a mate through a singles dating service.

Mortgages

Finding your first house or condominium could be easy, but obtaining enough financing may seem like a losing battle. It does not have to be that way if you know your limits and what to expect. Generally, you can determine the **mortgage** amount a bank would be willing to offer you. Calculate approximately one-third of your monthly gross income before taxes. Subtract from that amount all other debts, such as monthly car loan and credit card payments. This amount roughly equals the most you could spend on a monthly mortgage payment, according to a bank. For example, if interest rates are 10% and one-third of your monthly gross income, less debts, equals $600, your loan amount would be approximately $60,000. We will say it again: *approximately*. There is no special formula because banks also look at other factors. For example, banks will ask for a list of all your assets and liabilities. They will also ask how much you will spend on the down payment. Someone with $10,000 of assets and a down payment equal to 20% of the total purchase price will probably get a larger loan amount than someone who has $10,000 outstanding on a credit card and a 5% down payment.

When you are choosing a loan, it appears that everyone and their families sell mortgages. Banks handle mortgage loans as well as numerous mortgage companies. They are both eager to have your business, but that is not a guarantee that they will loan you the money. Choosing your banker or mortgage agent is similar to choosing a financial planner or broker. Ask around for names and trustworthy companies from your friends and family. This is especially important for choosing a mortgage broker because unfortunately, there are brokers who charge expensive up front fees and never produce a loan. For extra added safety, check with your state regulator for any complaints against a certain mortgage broker. Choose a representative you trust and who clearly explains each type of loan offered and the associated fees. Mortgage companies will usually offer lower interest rates than banks, however the points (fees) charged on the loan are generally higher.

In order to choose the mortgage that is right for you, it is important to find a representative who will take the time to clearly explain all available mortgages. In the following section, we will briefly describe two types of mortgages. For more detail, please consult a banker or mortgage agent.

A common type of mortgage is the 30-year **fixed interest rate**. This is popular during times of low interest rates because the borrower can lock into a low rate for the life of the mortgage (30 years). Another type of mortgage is an **adjustable-rate mortgage (ARM)**. These mortgages are popular during times of high interest rates because they often offer below-market interest rates for the first couple of years. After the initial period is over, the interest rate fluctuates for the remainder of the loan. They usually come with interest rate caps so the borrower is assured of not paying more than a fixed amount of interest. ARMs sometimes can be converted into fixed-rate mortgages during a specified time period. First-time home buyers may qualify for a federal government loan which can offer lower interest rates and a lower minimum down payment. Ask a banker for more details.

We've talked about the different kinds of mortgages, but what are the costs? Mortgage costs are commonly known as **closing costs**. A standard closing cost is referred to as **points** and is stated in a percentage. For example, two points on a loan represents fees equal to 2% of the loan amount. On a $100,000 loan, two points would be $2,000. Points vary from loan to loan and from institution to institution, but two points on a mortgage is not uncommon. This may seem high, however homeowners across the nation would be happy to just pay point fees. There are additional fees. The type and amount of closing costs will vary among institutions. For example, you may need to pay for an appraisal, credit report, title document, and a host of other services. The biggest gripe among homeowners is that one person could pay more in closing costs with the same loan amount than someone else. For more information on closing costs, ask for a free copy of the *U.S. Department of House and Urban Development (HUD) - Settlement Costs* at your local bank.

Prepayment

If you already have a mortgage, you may want to consider prepaying. This becomes beneficial when security investment interest rates are low and your mortgage interest rate is high. For example, if your mortgage is at 15% and your money could earn only 10% in a mutual fund, it would make sense to use extra income to pay off the mortgage. The easiest way to prepay is to take your monthly payment, divide by twelve and add that amount to your existing payment each month. If your monthly payment is $1,000, divide by twelve and you will get $83.33. You pay an additional $83.33 each month to your existing mortgage payment. At that rate, you can pay a 30 year mortgage in approximately 22 years. Why? Because the additional $83.33 is reducing principal at a much faster rate. Double check with your institution to be sure your mortgage does not have any prepayment penalties.

Refinancing

Refinancing is often easier than obtaining the initial mortgage — that is if your property and personal financial position has remained relatively constant. When interest rates drop, it is to your advantage to refinance. Banks will usually only refinance 80% of the appraised value of your property. If your property has decreased in value, you may not be able to refinance the full amount of your loan. Refinancing makes sense if you are planning to own your home for a extended period. Add up all the costs associated with refinancing (reappraisal, points, and fees), and divide by the number of months you plan on owning your home. Add this number to your new monthly payment. If it is still lower than your old monthly payment, refinance.

Raw Land

Buying raw land is often more difficult than it sounds. Generally, raw land is less expensive than a house, so many people think that they can qualify more easily for this type of loan. Unfortunately, that is far from the truth. There are few banks that will even lend money for raw land because the chance of loan default is higher than on a home mortgage. People will try not to default on their home mortgage because if they did they would not have a place to live. If they do default, the bank will resell the home. However with raw land, defaulting is not as detrimental to the land owner and the bank can be stuck with an asset they cannot easily resell. Banks will be more eager to lend you money for raw land if you intend to build a house within a certain time period. So how do people buy those 40 acres? You can either purchase land with cash or negotiate a payment schedule with the current owner. In other words, the original owner becomes your banker.

Other Investments in Real Estate

There are ways to invest in real estate without buying a single piece of property. **Real estate investment trusts (REIT)** are a way to invest in a portfolio of real estate properties. REITs are traded publicly and their assets are spread from shopping malls to office buildings. During unfavorable periods for the real estate market (high interest rates and low demand), these shares can be as volatile as stocks. They are best to buy when interest rates are low and demand is expected to grow. Master Limited Partnership (MLP) and Real Estate Limited Partnership (RELP) also present ways to invest in real estate. MLPs are publicly traded like stock, which makes the investment more liquid than a RELP. They usually have a $1,000 to $5,000 minimum investment. RELPs are private partnerships made up of a general partner, who organizes and manages the partnership, and limited partners, who contribute capital and assume no active role in day to day business. They usually require at least $20,000 and have no official secondary market. This makes RELPs hard to sell. Before tax laws were changed in 1986, RELPs were a very popular tax shelter. Today they are quiet investments that do not get a lot of attention.

Taxes

Having a home mortgage may be the best tax advantage. The interest paid on your home loan, plus property taxes, can be deducted from your federal income tax return. This makes a noticeable difference, especially during the first years of the loan when you are paying mostly interest and little equity. You can also deduct the one-time fees paid to the bank or mortgage broker in order to process the loan. Refinancing fees are tax deductible, but the deduction needs to be spread over the length of the loan. When you sell your primary residence, the capital gains resulting from the sale will not be taxed if you reinvest them in a residence of equal or greater value. A capital gain is the amount you make from selling your home. For example, if you bought your home for $100,000 and sold for $150,000, you would realize $50,000 in capital gains. You are also entitled to a one-time exemption from capital gains (up to a certain limit) after age 55.

The tax advantage, as well as building equity and gaining property appreciation, makes owning real estate a great investment.

CONCLUSION

Congratulations, you have made it through an entire book on investing. We hope that this book has helped take the mystery out of investing and has given you the courage to start spending today. In fact, we feel so strongly about the value of this book and its contents, that we are willing to go one step further. If there are any investments or concepts mentioned in this book that still come across like a foreign language, or if you need extra motivation, we encourage you to write directly to us: Orca Books Publishing, Questions for the Authors, P.O. Box 1138, Mercer Island, WA 98040-1138. Who knows, you may even stump us on a question. In that case, we would both learn because investing is a never ending topic.

There are always more concepts and strategies to learn. We would also love to know if you have other tips or references that are helpful to you.

We encourage you to read further on the topics that are of particular interest to you and your personal goals. OK, close this book, place it on the bookshelf next to your other reference materials, and always remember these last parting words: YOU CAN DO IT!!!!

REFERENCE DESK

GLOSSARY

12b-1 Fee - A marketing fee charged by some mutual funds. p.46

401(k) - A retirement savings plan set up by a company for its employees. Amounts grow tax-deferred until money is withdrawn. p.145

403(b) - A retirement savings plan set up by a public entity for its employees. Amounts grow tax-deferred until money is withdrawn. p.146

Adjustable-Rate Mortgage (ARM) - A loan with an initial fixed rate of interest which converts into a variable rate of interest at a later date. p.163

American Stock Exchange (AMEX) - The second largest stock exchange, located in New York City. p.62

Annual Report - A yearly report, compiled by a company, which contains product line information, financial information and company forecasts for the future. p.44 & 88

Asked Price - The price at which a stock will be sold to investors. p.73 See Bid Price.

Assets - The total value of everything a company owns. p.91

Auditor's Opinion - An auditor's opinion will either be qualified or unqualified. An unqualified opinion means that the auditor approves of the financial reports without condition. A qualified opinion will contain the auditor's reason for not giving the financial reports a clean bill of health. p.98

Baby Bond - A bond with a par value of generally less than $500. p.123

Back-End Loads or Exit Fees - An additional fee paid when shares of a mutual fund are sold. p.46

Balance Sheet - A financial report showing what is owned, what is owed, and what a company is worth on a particular date. p.91

Beta - a measure of the riskiness of a stock or equity mutual fund compared to the market average. p.51

Bid Price - The price at which a stock will be bought from investors. p.73 See Asked Price.

Blue Chip - Generic name for a stock of a stable, well established company with solid historical rates of return and a high prospect for long-term growth. p.68

Bond - A long-term debt of a corporation or government. See Corporate Bond, Municipal or State Bonds, U.S. Savings Bond, Junk Bond, Zero Coupon, and Treasuries for more detail. p.117

Book Value per Share - Stockholder's equity ÷ number of outstanding shares. p.80

Broker - Someone licensed to buy and sell securities. p.18

Buy Recommendation - Term used by analysts to recommend purchasing a stock. p.105

Call - An option for the right to buy a security. p.83 See Put.

Call Date - A provision in a bond that entitles the issuer to buy back the bond at an earlier date than the maturity date. p.124

Cash Value Life Insurance - Simple life insurance plus an investment program. Also called straight, whole, permanent or ordinary. p.152

Certificate of Deposit - Certificate for a bank deposit that earns a specific interest rate for a given time period. p.158

Closing Costs - Costs associated with obtaining a mortgage. p.163

Collateralized Bond - A bond that is backed by specific assets such as equipment or property. p.125

Commodity Futures - Anything traded on the futures market, such as coffee or orange juice. p.84

Common Shares Outstanding - The number of common stock shares held in the market of a particular company. p.79

Common Stock - Shares entitling the holder to receive dividends and voting privileges of the company. p.78

Compound Interest Rate - An interest rate that is computed upon the original investment plus all accumulated interest. p.11

Convertible Bond - A bond that can be traded in for shares of the same company's stock. p.128

Corporate Bond - Bond issued by a corporation. p.123 See Bond.

Coupon Rate - A bond's stated interest rate. p.118

Current Yield - The interest rate that a bond is currently earning. p.118

Debenture Bond - A bond that is backed by a company's financial health. p.125

Discount - The amount saved below an investment's par value. For example, if a bond in the open marketplace costs $800, it has a discount of $200 under the $1,000 par value. p.118 See Par Value.

Discount Brokerage - A brokerage firm which buys and sells securities at lower commissions to the investor than charged by a full service brokerage firm. p.64

Diversification - Spreading investor risk by holding a range of securities or particular investments. p.15 & 69

Dividend - An amount paid per share of stock owned by a shareholder. p.26 & 81

Dollar Cost Averaging - Investing a constant amount in securities at fixed time periods. p.17

Dow Jones Industrial Average (DJIA) - Commonly cited stock index which measures the combined effect of 30 different stocks. p.70

Earnings per Share (EPS) - (Net income minus preferred stock dividends) ÷ average number of common shares outstanding. p.79

Exercise Price - See Strike Price.

Exit Fees - See Back-End Loads.

Financial Planner - Someone licensed to buy and sell securities, who also offers financial planning advice. p.18

Fixed Interest Rate Mortgage - A loan with a fixed rate of interest that remains the same throughout the life of the loan. p.162

Full Service Brokerage - A brokerage firm which buys and sells securities and offers financial advice, but generally at higher commissions to the investor than those charged by a discount brokerage firm. p.64

General Obligation Bonds - Bonds that are backed by the issuer's general taxing power. p.133

Good Until Canceled - Keeps an order to buy or sell securities open and active until the investor cancels. p.73

Government Backed Securities - Investments backed by a federal government agency such as the Government National Mortgage Association (GNMA), Federal National Mortgage Association (FNMA), Federal Home Loan Mortgage Corporation (FHLMC), or the Student Loan Management Agency (SLMA). p.135

Hold Recommendation - Term used by analysts to recommend a neutral position in a stock. p.105

Income Statement - A report showing the revenue, costs, expenses, and the net income or net loss for a company. p.92 Also called Statement of Earnings.

Individual Retirement Account (IRA) - An investment for retirement which grows tax-deferred until money is withdrawn. p.144

Initial Public Offering (IPO) - The process by which new stocks are brought into the market place. p.67

Investing - The act of using money to create more money while minimizing risk. p.9

Investment Club - A formal club whose members discuss and decide how to invest their money. p.102

Junk Bond - Bond with a speculative grade rating of BB or Ba or lower on the *Standard & Poor's* or *Moody's* rating scale. p.55 Also called High Yield Bond.

Keough Plan - See Simplified Employee Pension Plan.

Liabilities - The total value of everything a company owes. p.91

Limit Order - An order to buy or sell securities at a specific price. p.73

Liquid Investment - An investment that is easily converted into money in a short time period. p.28

Liquidity of a Company - A company's financial ability to pay short-term debts such as rent or utility expense. In other words, a measure of a company's liquid investments compared to short-term debts. p.93

Load - An up front fee to purchase shares of a mutual fund stated in terms of a percentage. p.46 See No-Load.

Margin - Borrowing money based on the value of your portfolio, to buy securities. p.74

Market Share - The percentage of the market that a company controls. For example, in the car market, Ford's sales make up a certain percentage of the market as do Honda's and Saab's. Each percentage of the market is known as that company's market share. p.101

Market Value - Current price of a security. p.73

Maturity Date - The date at which a bond's purchase price is scheduled to be fully repaid. p.118

Mortgage - A loan, usually to buy property. p.161

Mortgage-Backed Securities - Investments backed by a pool of mortgages such as those of the Government National Mortgage Association (GNMA), Federal National Mortgage Association (FNMA), or the Federal Home Loan Mortgage Corporation (FHLMC). p.57 & 134 See Government Backed Securities.

Municipal or State Bonds - Bonds issued by a state or local government or government agency. p.16 & 131

Mutual Fund - An investment company that pools investors' money into a range of different securities, depending on the type of fund. p.39

Mutual Fund Family - A group of mutual funds with varying investment strategies that all belong to a single parent company. p.41

National Association of Investment Clubs - Organization that helps to establish investment clubs. ((313)-543-0612). p.102

National Association of Securities Dealers (NASD) - Organization that regulates licensed brokers and dealers. (1-800-289-9999). p.18

National Association of Securities Dealers Automated Quotations (NASDAQ) - System of computerized network trading for over-the-counter stocks. p.62

Net Asset Value (NAV) per share - The value of all investments owned by a mutual fund, less the liabilities, divided by the number of shares. p.48

Net Worth - Assets minus liabilities. See Stockholder's Equity. p.91

New York Stock Exchange (NYSE) - The oldest and largest stock exchange, located in New York City. p.62

No-Load - $0 in up front fees to purchase shares of a mutual fund. p.46 See Load.

Odd Lots - Less than 100 shares. p.74 See Round Lots.

Option Contract - A contract that gives the investor the right to buy or sell a security at a specified price within a specified time frame. p.83 See put, calls, and strike price.

Over-The-Counter (OTC) - Stocks not traded on one of the exchanges. p.62

Par Value - The money value assigned to a security. For most bonds, the par value equals $1,000. p.118

Points - A fee associated with obtaining a mortgage,

stated in terms of a percentage. p.163

Power of Compounding - See Compound Interest Rate. p.11

Preferred Stock - Shares that carry fixed dividends that must be paid before common stock dividends. Rarely includes voting privileges. p.78

Premium - The amount paid in excess of an investment's par value. For example, if a bond in the open marketplace costs $1,200, it has a premium of $200 over the $1,000 par value. p.118 See Par Value.

Price to Earnings Ratio (P/E) - Current price of stock ÷ earnings per share (EPS). p.79

Profitability - The excess income generated after costs. p.95

Portfolio - The combination and collection of securities held by an investor. p.16

Prospectus - A financial document containing company information, financials, and risk factors about a particular investment. p.67 & 89

Put - An option for the right to sell a security. p.83 See Call.

Qualified Opinion - See Auditor's Opinion.

Real Estate Investment Trusts (REIT) - Company, usually traded publicly, that manages a portfolio of real estate for its shareholders. p.165

Retained Earnings - Company earnings not paid out in dividends, distributed back to the company. p.91

Revenue Bonds - Bonds that are backed by a project's expected revenue. p.133

Risk - The possibility that an investment will not appreciate in value. p.14

Round Lots - Multiples of 100 shares. p.74 See Odd Lots.

Rule of 72 - 72 divided by the interest rate equals the number of years it will take to double an investment. p.11

Russell 2000 - Stock index which measures the combined effect of 2000 small company stocks. p.71

S&P 500 - Stock index which measures the combined effect of 500 stocks. p.71

Savings Bonds (U.S.) - See U.S. Savings Bonds.

Secondary Market - Exchanges and over-the-counter

markets where securities are bought and sold after the original issue. p.130

Selling Short - Selling shares of stock an investor does not own, in anticipation of the stock price falling. p.82

Shares - Unit of ownership in a corporation. p.91

Simplified Employee Pension Plan (SEP)/Keough - Retirement savings plans which grow tax-deferred until money is withdrawn. Designed for self-employed or employees of unincorporated businesses. p.146

Solvency of a Company - A company's financial ability to pay long-term debts such as future payments on a long-term loan. p.94

Spread - The difference between the bid and asked price. p.73 See Bid price and Asked price.

Statement of Changes in Net Assets - A mutual fund financial report showing the increase or decrease in net assets. p.89

Statement of Earnings - See Income Statement.

Statement of Operations - A mutual fund financial report that summarizes the net gain or loss on investments for that fund. p.89

Stock - Share in the ownership of a corporation. p.61

Stockholder/Shareholder/Shareowner - The owner of one or more shares of a corporation. p.91

Stockholders' Equity - The net worth or owner's interest of a company. In other words, the value of assets after creditors are paid. p.80 & 91 See Net Worth.

Stop Order - An order to sell securities placed below market value. p.73

Strike Price - The specified price stated in an option, at which an investor can buy or sell a security. Also called Exercise Price. p.83

Tax-Deferred Annuities (TDAs) - retirement investments which grow tax-deferred, until money is withdrawn. Usually sponsored by insurance companies. p.147

Tax-Deferred Investment - An investment in which taxes on the investment income are postponed until retirement, or until money is withdrawn from the investment. p.142

Term Life Insurance - Simple life insurance that does not contain cash value. p.142

Treasuries - Government issued Treasury bills, bonds, and notes, backed by the full faith of the U.S. government. The distinction between the three can be found in their length to maturities. p.127

U.S. Savings Bonds - U.S. government bonds sold in Series EE and Series HH Savings Bonds. p.137 See Bonds.

Unit Investment Trust - Consists of a constant portfolio of municipal bond investments. Similar to a municipal bond mutual fund. p.132

Unqualified Opinion - See Auditor's Opinion.

Yield to Maturity - The yield earned on a bond that incorporates the gain or loss on the bond's purchase price when it matures or is redeemed. p.118

Zero Coupon Securities - Heavily discounted, fixed income securities that pay no interest prior to maturity. p.139

General Investor References

Magazines

Business Week
Forbes
Fortune
Kiplinger's Personal Finance Magazine
Money
Newsweek
Time

Other Publications

Barron's Finance & Investment Handbook
Moody's Investors Services
Morningstar Mutual Funds
Morningstar 5 Star Investor
Robert Morris & Associates Annual Statement Studies
Standard & Poor's
Standard & Poor's The Outlook
Value Line Investment Survey
The Wall Street Journal

Computer Services

Compact Disclosure (CD) system
InfoTrac system

Quote References

Lynch, Peter. *Beating The Street*. New York, Simon & Schuster, 1993. (p.22)

Williamson, Ellen. *Wall Street Made Easy; An Unconventional Guide to Profitable Investing*. New York, Doubleday, 1965, p.37. (p.61)